WISDOM OF THE RISHIS

The Three Upanishads: Ishavasya, Kena & Mandukya

Other Titles by Sri M

The Little Guide to Greater Glory and a Happier Life

Wisdom of the Rishis:
The Three Upanishads: Ishavasya - Kena - Mandukya

Jewel in the Lotus: Deeper Aspects of Hinduism

How to Levitate and Other Secrets of Magic

The Upanishads - Katha, Prashna, Mundaka

Shunya: A Novel

On Meditation - Finding infinite Bliss & Power Within

The Journey Continues -
Sequel to Apprenticed to a Himalayan Master

Apprenticed to a Himalayan Master
A Yogi's Autobiography

The Autobiography of Sri M available in the following languages:
Hindi, Marathi, Tamil, Telugu, Kannada, Malayalam, Oriya, German, Russia, Bengali, Gujarati, Italian, Spanish

The Journey Continues available in the following languages:
Hindi, Marathi, Gujarati

To buy books and discourses by Sri. M online visit magentapress.in

WISDOM
OF THE
RISHIS

The Three Upanishads: Ishavasya, Kena & Mandukya

By
Sri M

edited by
Roshan Ali

with a foreword by
Dr. Karan Singh

Magenta Press

© The Author 2002

First printed 2002
This edition, 2012
Reprint-2014
Reprint-2016
Reprint-2017
Reprint-2018
Reprint-2019

ISBN: 978-81-910096-3-7

Book Design: J. Menon. www.grantha.com

Typeset: PKS

Published by Magenta Press and Publication Pvt. Ltd., No.9,1st Floor,Websters Road,Cox Town,Bangalore -560005. Tel: +91 9343071537.
info@magentapress.in, www.magentapress.in

My Param Guru Sri Guru Babaji.

My Guru Sri Maheshwaranath Babaji.

Contents

Preface

The contents of this book are the edited transcriptions of the discourses on the Upanishads by Sri M.

Minimum editing has been done to retain the style of the talks. The editor acknowledges the contribution of Ms. Uma Singh and Ms. Kamal Aswani in transcribing the discourses with care and attention.

The introductory portions might sound repetitious at times, but that could not be avoided, considering that the talks were given at different times to different people. It is suggested that these portions be re-read for a thorough comprehension of each Upanishad.

Editor

Foreword

The Upanishads represent the high watermark not only of Hindu Philosophy but of spiritual literature anywhere in the world. These marvellous discourses and dialogues between self-realized seers, known as Rishis, and one or more disciples, contain powerful and eloquent statements regarding the ultimate reality in its multifarious facets. They have been well described as providing an 'ecstatic slide show of reality, a privileged glimpse of the unitive vision in which all thing are one in a world aflame with God'. They contain some of the most eloquent passages such as – 'I have seen that Great Being shining like a thousand suns beyond the darkness; it is only by knowing that being that we can achieve immortality' and again, 'Hear O children of immortal bliss, you are born to be united with the Divine; follow the path of the illumined ones and be united with the Supreme Being'.

The universal truths articulated in the Upanishads have formed the basis for numerous commentaries down through the centuries, beginning with the luminous insights of Adi Shankaracharya. In our own times Sri Aurobindo, Sri Krishnaprem, Dr Radhakrishnan, Swami Ranganathananda, Eknath Ishwaran and other great seers and sages have produced commentaries and interpretations on various Upanishads. The Upanishads are enduring and unfailing sources of inspiration, and their impact grows with each successive reading. One of my favourites is the *Mundaka* which I have translated and upon which I have attempted a short commentary.

The author of this book, Sri Mumtaz Ali, popularly known as 'M', has spoken extensively upon the Upanishads, based on his personal experience. The fact that a person born a Muslim should have such a deep insight into the Hindu tradition proves once again that the spiritual path accepts no boundaries. The three Upanishads upon which M has commented are among the most important – the *Ishavasya*, which is always given pride of place in any list of Upanishads, the *Mandukya* which expounds the deeper symbolism of the sacred symbol *Aum*, and the *Kena* where we have the marvellous allegory of the Devas who thought they had won a victory, whereas actually it was the victory of the divine *Brahman*. In this Upanishad we come across Shiva and Yaksha, whose identity the Devas are unable to comprehend, and are also introduced to Uma, Haimavati, the many splendoured daughter of the Himalayas, who appears as the mediator between the Devas and the Supreme *Brahman*.

In these talks M has expounded in a clear and cogent fashion various aspects of these three great texts. I have pleasure in commending this book to spiritual seekers and students of Hinduism around the world.

Dr. Karan Singh

A Profile of 'M'

The boy was a little more than 9 years old when he saw the strange being. He was the son of a Deccani Muslim family, settled in Trivandrum, the beautiful capital of Kerala. Having heard stories of angels coming down to bless Mohammed and other prophets and saints from his devout grandmother, he thought at first that it was an angel.

One evening, the boy was wandering around the courtyard of his house in Vanchiyoor, doing nothing in particular. At the far end of the courtyard, he saw someone standing under the jackfruit tree. The stranger gestured to the boy to come forward. The boy felt no fear whatsoever, and was eager to go closer to the stranger.

The stranger was tall, fair and well-built and was bare-bodied except for a piece of loin cloth worn around his waist. He put his right hand on the boy's head and asked with kindness, "Do you remember anything?" in Hindi. To the boy's answer that he didn't, the stranger said in Deccani, "You will understand later. You will not meet me for many years after this, but you will have to finish the studies that you have left incomplete. You will not be allowed to tell anyone about me until the time is ripe. Go home now." With that he vanished.

That was the first initiation. Two years later, while playing hide and seek, the boy experienced what may be described in yogic terms as *Keval Kumbhak* – the suspension of inhalation and exhalation. Bliss filled his heart. The breathing resumed in a few minutes.

Soon he could get into it at will with a deep sigh. The bliss that he experienced convinced him that a greater world existed within his being – a world of spiritual bliss.

In his outward appearance he was just like any other boy except that he loved religious scriptures and philosophy – no matter of which religion, devotional songs and discussions on God, saints and sages.

When he was eleven, he used to go in the evenings to a certain house which belonged to one Mr. Pillai, whose nephew and son-in-law tutored him in mathematics. One evening he entered Pillai's house as usual and found himself face to face with a venerable, sturdy man of about sixty, clean shaven and with closely cropped silver grey hair, wearing a half sleeved shirt and loin cloth, sitting cross-legged on a bench. The room smelled of incense.

"Hello!" said the old man in Malayalam, "Come, come. Don't be afraid."

'M' walked up to him. The man patted his back and caressed his neck and head and said, "Umm. Good! Everything will be all right in good time."

Again the breathless condition and greater bliss. 'M' stood up and went straight home. The guidance had begun. He was the first of the great souls 'M' was to meet in the course of his spiritual journey.

Much later 'M' came to know that the man was a great self-realised soul who lived in 'Atma Bhava' and was simply called Pujapura Swami since he lived in Pujapura. He was unmarried but not a formal monk. In his youth he had been initiated into yogic practices by a great teacher and ever since had lived a model life, his heart absorbed in the blissful, Supreme Brahman while he performed his duties like an ordinary mortal.

'M' also learnt that the Swami used to hold midnight Satsangs on certain days, which a great sanyasin, who had renounced even his loin-cloth, would sometimes attend. Pujapura Swami was not known outside a small circle because he forbade propaganda.

When 'M' was seventeen, the *sanyasin* was no more, but a friend handed over a compilation of his teachings to 'M' which was privately circulated. It contained the essence of *Vedanta* in very simple language.

By then, the knowledge that 'M' needed from time to time as he progressed on the path began to come to him automatically. His father had borrowed B. K. S. Iyengar's *Light on Yoga* from a friend of his (his father was never an orthodox Muslim). 'M' read it through. A yoga teacher, Sri Sharma, gave him his initial lessons on yogasanas and Surya Namaskaras.

'M' met Swami Tapasyananda of the Ramakrishna Mission, a direct disciple of Sarada Devi. He was then the head of Ramakrishna Mission at Trivandrum. The librarian at the Trivandrum Public Library kept 'M' well supplied with the works of Vivekananda. He chanced to read Swami Chinmayananda's *Japa Yoga* and *Gayatri* and he began to chant the Gayatri Mantra. A Tantric instructed him in certain mantras and lent him Sir John Woodroffe's *Serpent Power*. He read many other books – the *Upanishads*, the *Gita*, Yogic texts and *Vedanta* included. He discovered that Sanskrit was not too difficult to understand.

Side by side with gaining theoretical knowledge, he meditated for long hours, especially at midnight. He had merely to shut his eyes and concentrate on the lotus of the heart to enter into Keval Kumbhak and experience tremendous bliss and extraordinary visions of divine lights and voices. Sometimes terrifying visions would flit across his mind but they would pass and he would once again be filled with ecstasy.

Then he met a great person known as Chempazanthi Swami. The Jesuits had started their first Loyola Junior College at Sreekaryam in Trivandrum and 'M' was among the first batch of pre degree students. A few kilometers away was the remote village of Chempazanthi which is the birth place of Sri Narayana Guru, the great reformer-saint. Close to Chempazanthi is Chenkotkonam where the Swami lived.

He was a tea-shop owner turned saint. A great *bhakta* of Rama, he was known to have lived like Hanuman for a long time, eating nuts and climbing trees. He was fond of bhajans and kirtans. When 'M' met him in his hut, he was thin and frail and very delicate looking. Crowning his ever-smiling face was a great chunk of wound-up matted hair and he smelled of Vibhuti. Taking a pinch of ash, he touched M's forehead with it, popped a couple of grapes into his mouth and said, 'Umm, needs to ripen, will ripen. Do bhajans.' 'M' meditated for a few minutes, prostrated and left the place.

Those days 'M' had a close Brahmin friend whose father worshipped Sai Baba of Shirdi. The moment 'M' saw Baba's picture , an irresistible desire to know about Baba's life rose in him. The next day Mr. Subramanya Iyer, an advocate, who was his friend's landlord, gave him a copy of the *Life of Sai Baba of Shirdi* by Narasimha Swamiji." Then he lent 'M' *Sai Sat Charita*. He fell in love with the great Faqir.

At this time 'M' heard from a friend of his who was a medical student (he is now a neuro-surgeon) about a lady Avadhuta called Mai Ma, who lived on the Kanyakumari beach. She was reputed to be over a hundred years old and no one could say where she came from or what language she spoke. The few words she said sounded very much like Bengali.

'M' went to see her alone. Kanyakumari is close to Trivandrum. He reached Kanyakumari a little before noon. He walked from the bus stand and came to the entrance of the Devi Temple. He casually walked across the rocky beach and there she was. A woman who looked to be in her sixties, she wore absolutely no clothes, her face a typically Bengali face, glowing, ageless eyes, smiling. She sat on one of the rocks with a circle of street dogs around her forming a security ring. The dogs snarled when they saw 'M.'

Mai Ma scolded the dogs using peculiar sounds and they dispersed and sat at a distance. She motioned to 'M' to sit down. He sat down on a rock. She pointed to the dosas that he had with him and said something. He gave her the dosas. She fed the dogs some, ate two herself and returned a few to him. He closed his eyes and tried to tune in with her vibrations. After a long time he opened his eyes. She was still there. Giving a broad smile she said, "*Jao, jao, thik…*" The last word could not be made out.

When Paramahamsas say "Go", one has no business to stay. 'M' prostrated and came away. After visiting the Vivekananda Rock, 'M' returned to Trivandrum.

He was made aware of the significance of Mai Ma's darshan the following morning. Tired after meditating for a long time in the night, he could not bring himself to be up at dawn. As he slept deeply he had a wonderful and vivid dream. In the dream he was a mendicant with matted hair and wearing only a 'kaupin,' sitting in padmasana and meditating under a Banyan tree which stood in the middle of a junction where four paths crossed each other. The jungle all around was thick.

A faint sound made him open his eyes, and from one of the paths he saw Mai approaching with a stick in her hand. She was huge, much larger than life-size. Reaching the place where he sat she touched his chin and said, "Give me something to eat."

He told her, "Mai Ma, I have only two grains of parched rice hidden in my matted hair."

She said, "Give me."

Without hesitation he gave the rice to her. She said to him, "Are you hungry?" He said "Yes, but you eat it Ma." She ate with great relish and turning to him said, "Your hunger is for a different thing. Close your eyes."

He closed his eyes. She pressed the middle of his forehead hard with what seemed to be her thumb. An ocean of bliss filled his whole being with its centre in the forehead. Every cell of his being was suffused with it. He lost his body consciousness. Only the other existed.

Then he woke up. The dream vanished, but O! How fortunate! The bliss remained. He was like a drunken man who had had his fill. Slowly he sat up and stretched his legs and carefully went to the bathroom, afraid that he would fall. In a few minutes he got full control over his body and mind but the stream of bliss continued in the core of his being. It has since remained with him. At times low, at times high, but always there.

Already acquainted with the teachings of the Sufis by attending meetings of local Sufi groups and meeting some of the Amirs of the different Tariqats, he went at last to a gem among Sufis.

That was Kaladi Mastan who lived naked on the beach near Bimapalli in Trivandrum. He was drinking a cup of tea given by a follower when 'M' first saw him. He smiled and gave 'M' the rest of the tea. Then he said, "Big thief came to steal the treasure. Take it legitimately." Then he lit a cigarette and said, "Smoke." 'M' smoked. Then he took it back. 'M' sat and meditated before him. He covered M's head with sand and further cleared the conduits. He behaved like a mad man and many even thought he was mad, but he was a priceless gem and the few who were serious, knew. He is physically no more now. Many visit his tomb.

Not very far from there lived Poontharasami, another God-intoxicated person with matted hair, who too was mistaken by many to be a madman. When 'M' visited him, he suddenly stood up and kicked 'M' on his chest. That was a timely kick. It cleared the passage through which the mighty energy travels.

When 'M' went to thank him a month later, he had vanished, nobody knew where. An impressive looking fraud, who claimed to have been his closest disciple, tried to influence 'M.' The poor chap did not realize that 'M' could read him like an open book.

When he was nineteen, 'M' made up his mind to go to the Himalayas. First he went to Madras by train, spent sometime in the Theosophical Society, then took a train to Delhi. From Delhi he went to Hardwar. From Hardwar he decided to walk.

All the money was finished. He had no intention of writing back home for help or even to let them know where he was. He knew he would be looked after, that the minimum needs of the body would be taken care of by the great powers that run the universe, and he was right. Of course, at certain times, he was tested thoroughly but in the end everything was fine. On foot he covered the entire journey from Rishikesh to Uttarkashi, to Gangotri, Yamunotri, from Batwari to Kedar via Buda Kedar, then to Badrinath.

At Rishikesh, he decided to stay in the Divine Life Society and continue his studies and meditation. It is a lovely place for *sadhaks*.

The Ganges flows nearby. Yoga is taught in the Ashram. The senior swamis are a great help and when one has time, one can wander around and meet sadhus of various sects. Satsang is most important for a sadhak.

That pilgrim-season found 'M' walking again to Badrinath – sometimes on the common pilgrim routes, sometimes through forests, staying in roadside *dharmashalas* and *chattis* and many a time in forest hermitages beside the river. On his way to Badrinath, he visited Vasishta Guha and Arundhati Cave. He gathered much food for the soul.

Reaching Badrinath after many days' journey, he first slept in the choultry. It was quite cold and his single blanket was insufficient, but he was in no mood to seek help. Those were the days when the fire of spirituality burned so bright that everything else, even the bare necessities – food, clothes and shelter – melted into insignificance. A highly intoxicating, ecstatic mood came over him in the great Himalayas. He attributed this, as also his intense sadhana to the presence of highly evolved beings in these regions. He hoped to meet some of them.

His physical difficulties were solved by the arrival of a Brahmachari whom he had met earlier in the Divine Life Society. He was an experienced pilgrim who had travelled many times. Quickly he found 'M' an independent kutir and persuaded him to stay there. He also got 'M' a couple of blankets and a wooden plank to sleep on; he also arranged with the Nepali Dharmashala for his food. He introduced 'M' to the Rawalji, the chief priest of Badrinath, and took him on a sort of conducted tour on most evenings.

In Badrinath as in other pilgrim centres, there were beggars wearing saffron, others wearing the holy robes to make a living, even sadhus who stole *kamandalus* and blankets from each other.

Genuine yogis and *paramahamsas* also existed side by side, mingling with the common crowd and often deliberately pretending to be one of them.

Eager to see more of such souls and learning that they lived beyond Badrinath and on the other side of Narayan Parvat, 'M' decided to travel further. Without informing anyone, one morning he started off with his *kamandalu*, staff and blanket.

He had earlier explored about a kilometer of that road on his previous visit to Badrinath but beyond that the territory was unknown. After about six or seven kilometres of not easy climbing, he reached the confluence of the Saraswati and the Alakananda, called Keshav Prayag. Close to this was the cave, which, an old sanyasin had once told him, was the Vyasa Guha.

'M' walked beyond the Vyasa Guha to explore the other caves in the vicinity. He had walked through the rocky terrain for a long time when he realized that it would soon grow dark. Filled with doubt, fear and hunger, and disappointed about not finding any *mahatmas*, 'M' began to walk down towards the Mana village. On the way back, when he reached the Vyasa Guha, he found that a *dhuni* was brightly burning at the mouth of the cave. A strange force seemed to make his feet heavy. His heart overflowed with bliss but his legs would not move away from the cave. He took this as a signal and walked towards the cave. From inside the cave came a voice calling him by the name "Madhu". Seeing this young man, the long-haired, bare-bodied, tall man patted on his left shoulder with great affection and asked him to sit. At that instant, 'M' recognised the person whom he had once met in the backyard of his house under the jackfruit tree. He had found his guru, his father, his mother, all in one.

'M' spent three and a half years with his Master travelling all over the Himalayas. The Master advised him to go back to the plains and lead a normal life and begin teaching when commanded to do so. The

Master promised to keep in touch. The Master had thoroughly over-hauled his thought-process and brought about a lasting change in his consciousness.*

According to the Master's advice, 'M' went back to the plains, met many spiritual teachers and godmen, travelled all over India, took up difficult jobs to earn a living and to "see the world at close quarters," as the Master put it. He also lived for a short while like a very materialistic-minded person, and found that compared to the spiritual life and its greater vistas, the life of the worldly man is almost nothing. The joys of the spirit are much superior and it is the worldly man who renounces real happiness that springs from the heart.

But all that experience was necessary to tackle the worldly-wise who would say, "Oh! what do you know of the bliss of sensory experiences. You have not had any."

Now 'M' feels that he can say with confidence, "Friend, I know, and there is nothing to go ga ga about."

Off and on he had attended the talks of J. Krishnamurti in Madras and elsewhere and read most of his literature. Finally he met him and had a private discussion for forty-minutes after which he decided to stay on in the Krishnamurti Foundation for sometime. The Master had said that Krishnamurti would be the last of the important persons that 'M' would meet as part of his education and had instructed him to pay particular attention to everything that 'K' did and how the organisation would function when he lived and after his death. 'M' had close contact with J. Krishnamurti during the last two years of his life and was made a Trustee of the Krishnamurti Foundation, which position he resigned after five years.

After K's death 'M' married Sunanda whom he had met in Vasant Vihar, the headquarters of the Krishnamurti Foundation, and became a householder.

---

* The psychic channels in the spine and brain were opened up and the dormant energies activated so that the contact between the mind and the higher Consciousness was re-established.

He now feels that no one can say to him, "Well, brother, it is alright for you to say, 'lead a spiritual life and live in the world etc.', because you are unmarried ..." and so on. 'M' lives with his wife and two children. "In fact, it is the best thing to do in this period of the earth's existence, for *Sanyasa* is only for the rarest of the rare," says 'M.' With the blessings of his Himalayan Master and by strenuous sadhana 'M' has transcended theories and scholarship and is established in higher consciousness.

The Master had said to 'M,' "Do not advise people if you cannot follow the same advice. Do not talk on something if you have no personal experience." Wonderful teaching indeed! If only teachers follow this teaching what a lovely world this would be!

Gp. Capt. (Retd.) Ratnakar Sanadi

(For a detailed account of Sri M's life, please read his autobiography *Apprenticed to a Himalayan Master – A Yogi's Autobiography and The Journey Continues*, a sequel to the autobiography)

—ᘻ—

Ishavasya Upanishad

he *Ishavasya Upanishad*, which is also known as *Ishopanishad*, is one of the smallest of the *Upanishads*. Yet, it is one of the most important *Upanishads*. From time immemorial sages have not only gained wisdom through their study but have also understood and experienced the Truth, and then given their experiences in the form of the *Upanishads*.

It would be better if a small introduction is given to the very meaning of the word, '*Upanishad*,' before commencing study of the *Ishavasya Upanishad*.

The *Upanishads* are the *Jnana-kanda* – the 'wisdom-section' – of the four Vedas: *Rig, Yajur, Sama* and *Atharva*. Each has three portions – first the *Samhitas*, second the *Brahmanas*, and finally the *Aranyakas* and the *Upanishads*. The *Samhitas* are generally hymns sung in praise of Gods; the *Brahmanas* generally deal with the ritualistic performance of ceremonies; then we have the *Aranyakas* and the *Upanishads*.

The *Upanishads* as well as the *Aranyakas* were taught in forest-hermitages, not because the *rishis* were afraid to live in cities, but because being away from the mad rush of civilization provided an atmosphere conducive to the understanding of the scriptures. And so, they are called *Aranyakas* because they were taught in the forest-academies of the *Rishis* who lived with their students in the ambience of beautiful woods, mountains and rivers.

The *Upanishads* are also called '*Vedanta*' because they come at 'the end of the *Vedas*' – *Veda antah*; that is one view. The other view is that if you have studied the *Upanishads*, you have finished the study of all the *Vedas*. Therefore, it is also '*Vedanta*' – 'the end of the Vedas.' One view is factual and the other philosophical.

What does the word *Upanishad* mean? The word *Upanishad* has been divided into three parts: *upa – ni – shad*. '*Upa*' means 'to go closer, to move closer, to move nearer to.' So in this case, it means 'to move nearer to the truth' in the philosophical context. In the practical context, 'to move nearer to the teacher' means, to give attention to what is being said. When you say, 'move nearer to somebody,' it means dissolve the obstacles which are between you and that somebody, so that the listening takes place properly, without reservations.

The last syllable, '*shad*,' indicates, 'to sit.' When you sit down physically, it means that you are ready to listen. Of course, there were great sages who could meditate standing, but for most people, sitting is associated with settling down physically, in the mental frame of, 'O.K., I've done my work, now let me sit down, relax and try to understand the deeper aspects of reality.' This 'sitting-down' is *shad*. But when one physically sits down and the mind wanders, thinks about something else, then that cannot be called *shad*. There is a deeper meaning to *shad* – 'the settling down of the mind.' The mind needs to be completely receptive to what is being said.

Now the syllable '*ni*', which connects *upa* and *shad* – indicates the level of sitting. *Ni* Means 'sitting down at a level lower than that of the teacher,' which of course is not a physical level but a mental level. This *ni* means that the student or the listener realizes there are things to be learnt, things of which he knows little, and therefore decides, 'Let me listen to somebody who knows.' That, in some way, curtails the egotistic feeling that comes up often when we listen, which says, 'I know that, I know what he is saying, I know everything.' So, this *ni* indicates the humility required to listen and understand. It is not necessary that we should always bow down to the teacher or fall at his feet. These are only external marks of respect which may or may not be genuine. Humility means the understanding or awareness that one does not know at all, or that perhaps there is more to know.

Confucius has this wonderful example. He asks, "When you use a bowl, do you use the empty space or the walls that surround it? You use the space, because without the space nothing can be received. If it is already full, nobody can give you anything."

So, this sitting down in voluntary humility, not imposed humility, and listening in the mood of 'let me understand what is being said' – that somewhat defines *ni*.

So, bringing all the three parts – *upa-ni-shad* – together means that the teacher and the student, or the speaker and the listener sit down together, with the intention of moving closer to the Supreme Truth. This is done with complete humility on both sides and with complete intent to listen and understand, putting away all the obstacles to listening. This is the meaning of the word *Upanishad*.

One of the *shanti mantras* of another Upanishad defines this clearly:

Sahanavavatu sahanaubhunaktu saha veeryam karavavahai
Tejasvinavadhitamastu ma vidvishavahai.

'Let both the student and the teacher co-operate; together be protected, together be nourished.' The word used is, 'together.' 'Let us not quarrel among each other' – *ma vidvishavahai*.

The shanti mantra, the invocatory verse of the Ishavasya Upanishad, may, on the face of it, sound confusing or even meaningless. The *mantra* is:

Purnamadah purnamidam purnat purnamudachyate
Purnasya purnamaadaya purnamevavashishyate.

If we translate as well as we can into English it would read thus:
Purnamadah: 'That is complete.'
Purnamidam: 'This is complete.'
Purnamadah purnamidam 'That is complete, this is complete.'
Purnat purna mudachyate – 'From that completeness comes this completeness' or 'That completeness is the source of this completeness.'
Purnasya purnamaadaya – 'If we take away this completeness from that completeness...'
Purnamevavashishyate: 'Only completeness remains.'

4

Like all *Upanishadic* statements, this too does not have only one shade of meaning. That is why there have been several translators and commentators of the *Upanishads,* and each person has approached it stressing that particular point that appeals to him, or one that would interest a certain section of his students.

One of the philosophical interpretations of *purnamadah purnamidam,* especially because it comes in the beginning of the *Ishavasya Upanishad,* is that the Supreme Reality, which has been variously described in the *Upanishad* as the *Supreme Brahman, Para Brahman,* The Ultimate Truth, is 'that Supreme Reality which is Complete'. This means it is *purna,* because it is always full; it does not crave for anything; it is by itself independent and self-existing, permanent, remaining when everything else perishes. It is that Supreme Reality which knows no darkness but only effulgence, which is *nirmala* – free of impurities or imperfections. Therefore it is perfect, complete, and full.

That is understandable, but is also speculative since we don't know what that Supreme Brahman is. Now comes the phrase *purnamidam* – 'This is also Complete'. One comes across such sentences in the *Ishavasya Upanishad* as one proceeds, which would appear to be intended deliberately to confuse, but they are not. One has to look at it a little carefully. So by saying 'That Supreme Truth is complete' and 'This is complete', rishis are trying to take away the line of differentiation between 'That' and 'This'.

The *Chandogya Upanishad* says '*sarvam kalvidam brahma*' – 'All this is Brahman.'

All this that you see is the Truth – the only thing is, it is veiled. You remove the veil, and all differences disappear. Then 'this' becomes no different from 'that *Brahman*.' There is no differentiation between This and That, because differentiation is caused by the dividing mind. 'That is Complete, This is Complete.' Therefore, there is no way anything can be taken out or separated. We may think we are separating, but we actually are not.

Purnamevavashishyate – even if we think we are separating, 'That remains complete and *purna*.' There is no way it can be separated, split, divided. It is the ultimate, supreme message of absolute unity. That is one aspect. The other aspect is the physical. It is a description of the sum total of energy that can neither be decreased nor increased. Energy can neither be created nor destroyed. It can change from one form to another, but you cannot make it disappear, because the sum total remains constant. This is the physical aspect.

If we come to the psychological, the inner aspect of this particular *mantra*, we have to touch upon a subject which the *Upanishad* may not directly talk about, but is a part of personal *sadhana*. We are now venturing into the subtle subject of the inner energy called the *kundalini*. Now, the meditator, the person who wishes to go into the examination of the deeper aspects of the *Upanishad*, is told that there is an energy in all human beings which remains inactive in most cases, and the process of *sadhana* is that by which this potential energy is awakened. So long as this energy is inactive, it is potential energy. It is converted into active or kinetic energy through *sadhana*.

Before this energy becomes inactive, it does all the work of reproduction and growth. The whole growing-up of the organism, from the embryo to the state of a full-grown person, is done by this energy. And after it has done all its work, it descends to a psychic location, which is identified physically at the end of the spinal column, coils up, and becomes inactive. But, even after doing all this work, nothing is reduced from it. The energy is dormant, and remains forever as it was. All its work has been done, the organism has grown, yet nothing has been taken away, reduced or subtracted from this energy. It remains ready to be awakened by the proper person, at the proper time. This is one of the ways by which one could interpret this *mantra*. There may be many more. But now we go directly into the *Ishavasya Upanishad*.

Ishavasya Upanishad is part of the *Yajur Veda*. Among the *Upanishads* attached to the *Yajur Veda* it is, though short, one of the most important *Upanishads*. The first *shloka* of this *Upanishad is*:

SHLOKA 1

ishavasyam idam sarvam yat kincha jagatyaam jagat
tena tyaktena bhunjitha ma gridhah kasya svid dhanam.

Isha – 'that Supreme Lord – that Supreme Being,' *Ishwara*; *vasyam* – 'pervades'; *idam* – 'here'; *sarvam-*'everything.'

The *Upanishad* does not say, *Ishavasyam sarvam* – it adds a word *idam* – *Ishavasyam idam sarvam* – which means, 'It pervades everything, here and now.'

There is the usual blame laid at the door of *Upanishadic* teaching, that it is an 'other worldly teaching,' something to take up after one becomes old, or may be in the next birth. This is not true. *Ishavasyam idam sarvam-* 'that Supreme Being pervades everything' – here and now!

Yat kincha jagatyam jagat – 'It pervades all that moves, and also all that does not move,' which means, not only living beings, but also non-living things. Now, this distinction of 'that which moves' and 'that which does not move.' is a very relative distinction, because from the point of view of the physicist, there is nothing that does not move. A piece of stone or a piece of metal does not move for us, because we see it as static. We do not see what is happening inside – but from the point of view of Physics – quantum physics or practical physics – everything is in constant motion. There is nothing that stops. So, that Supreme Being, *Isha*, pervades everything here, 'that which appears to move and also that which does not appear to move.'

Then the *rishi* says, if the Supreme Being pervades 'that which moves and that which does not move,' whose wealth is all this, anyway? *Ma gridhah kasya svid dhanam*, which means, 'Who does all this belong to? You? Me? To whom does the cosmos belong? If the Supreme Being pervades everything, then what property belongs to whom?'

Therefore he says, 'tena tyaktena bhunjitha' – 'therefore, let go and rejoice!' Now, this is, on the face of it, a contradictory statement. Normally, rejoicing is linked with having more and more.

One needs to acquire more things in order to rejoice, is it not? But here is a contradictory statement which says, 'Let go and rejoice!' It can only be understood by someone who has given up something and found the relief, the joy in doing so! Otherwise, this cannot be understood.

The Upanishad says, that 'letting go' can be done only when it is understood that the Supreme Being pervades everything. If it pervades everything, then the human being becomes self-sufficient. There is nothing which needs to be added to the human being from outside. The rejoicing is in the understanding that your very Self is not different from that Isha, that Supreme Being.

Of course, when one is alive, one eats, drinks, and consumes, but deep in the consciousness, it is to be understood that the true rejoicing is a state of mind and is not dependent upon what you acquire or enjoy. 'Rejoicing' is more to do with the inner state than outer possessions. As one acquires fame, status and a bank balance, then automatically more needs are created and one requires more. This goes on. It is an unending process. It is not that we should give up everything and become sanyasins – No! What is being said is that as we watch, as we become aware of this unending process of acquiring, we realize that there is a state of mind which is independent of all this. That comes about only when one practically realizes what has been written here – Ishavasyam idam sarvam.

For example, if one is eating tasty food, what happens in the process? One spoons the food into one's mouth and enjoys it. Now, who is it who enjoys it? Where is the enjoyment taking place? Is it taking place in the mouth or, is it taking place inside the person?

What happens is that when there is enjoyment, it seems as if it springs from a reservoir of enjoyment within the person, which can be activated by the sensory organs coming in contact with that particular *padartha* or food item. When the sense organs are in touch with a particular taste or aroma or sight, then, from the inner reservoir of joy, a little bit is tapped. It comes out, it manifests itself and one says 'I am enjoying the food.'

The *rishis* declare that the reservoir of all enjoyment, which manifests itself in small portions as in the last example, is all within. You may call it *hridaya*, you may call it the 'inner consciousness,' you may call it *atma*. It is within! If you can understand that, then you can enjoy everything at once. It comes about not through craving for enjoyment but by understanding that the craving has to cease, or by understanding that the craving has no end.

Suppose you desire something, you work very hard in order to acquire it. What happens after that? You spend hours guarding it, wondering if the doors are properly locked at night because somebody may steal it. Whatever we acquire – and we are taking about not only physical objects, but also of status, name, fame – we are always afraid of losing it. So, to hold on to an image, to hold on to an object, after acquiring it, is itself a conflict. If it slips away, the happiness due to acquiring it also slips away at that moment. When the process of trying to hold on to what one acquires starts, automatically the happiness of acquiring it is diluted. Or, one may acquire something, keep it and say, 'I must enjoy it from tomorrow,' but in the night one might die in his sleep. These are all possible. Anything can happen. It is not pessimism.

So, when one realizes this impermanence of life and when one begins to wonder whether there is anything permanent at all, the *rishis* step in and say that 'There is something in you which is permanent, which is in yourself. You don't have to search for it outside. Your search for happiness, which the whole world searches for, is actually the search for this Supreme *Isha* – but in the wrong direction!'

The *rishis* who have taught the *Upanishads* say, 'This wonderful thing is here, inside you. It is for this that you are searching!' But even if you say this one hundred times to somebody, the understanding will come only when one is ready for it. There is no other way. Somebody may say, 'No, I don't want to listen to all this, let me enjoy', or 'I don't want to bother about searching within.' That is fine. But an intelligent and serious person need not put his finger into the fire, get burnt, and then understand that the fire is hot. He can see others burning their fingers, and learn from it!

The *Upanishad* says, '*Ishavasyam idam sarvam*' – 'that Supreme Being pervades everything here.' *Yat kincha jagatyam jagat* – 'That which moves and That which does not move.' Actually, the word *jagat*, which we call the world, comes from the root, 'to move.'

Tena tyaktena bhunjitha – 'therefore, let go and rejoice! Let go!' Don't get caught up in this circus. Let go and enjoy yourself – rejoice! *Ma gridhah kasya svid dhanam* – Whose wealth is this anyway?

SHLOKA 2

kurvann eveha karmani jijivishet shatam samaah
evam tvayi nanyatheto asti na karma lipyate nare

The *rishi* says:
If one understands, (even theoretically), if one begins to look into what has been proposed in the first *shloka*, then 'one can live performing *karmas* for a hundred years.' Again, this *Upanishad* does not say, 'Stop all your *karmas* and run away to the forest.' It says that if you understand, and if you are ready to look into what has been said in the first *shloka*, then you can do *karmas* for a hundred years and lead your life – that is the only way.

Nanyatheto asti – 'that is the only way.' There is no other way by which you can live a full life, performing all karmas on this earth, and yet – *na karma lipyate nare* – not be affected by the effect of these *karmas*.

Now we must clarify this. When the *rishi* says, *Na karma lipyate nare*, without the *karmas* affecting you, it does not mean that you will not suffer. It means that, having understood that your essential nature is that *Isha*, which pervades everything, you will not be affected by karmas. Everybody goes through difficulties. It is not that saints lead wonderful lives without any physical problems. We have known of great saints who have suffered with cancer and other diseases. But while an ordinary man is finished, he finds he has nowhere to turn, the realized person finds that his true identity, the atman, is not affected by any of these things, and therefore he carries on with a smile. Life, death, problems, hurt, pain – everything is common to all human beings as long as one has a physical body. But the inner-mind, subtle-mind, which is centered on the *atman*, lives through even the worst of pain with great bliss. This is the secret.

Therefore, the *rishi* says that you can do all your *karmas* and live for a hundred years, without the *karmas* having any effect on you, provided you understand the import of the first *shloka*.

SHLOKA 3

asurya nama te loka andhena tamasavrutah
tams te pretyabhigacchanti ye ke cha atma hano janah

Asurya nama te loka andhena tamasa. This means, 'There are some worlds which are enveloped in darkness to which those of demonic nature go.' 'Demonic' does not mean people who look like devils or monsters. It means demonic nature. Demonic means 'one who denies the performance of the Inner Self,' 'one who denies the Self.' So, *asurya nama te loka* means 'Those who deny the Inner Reality, who think that this world is all that is real, that there is nothing more than what they see around them – they go into worlds of darkness.'

11

Even without going into the philosophical aspect, one can understand this. There are people who think that all that there is, is this world. There is nothing else, there is no inner-world, there is no *atma*. We had such believers in ancient India – the *charvaka*. They said, 'Any time you may die – so eat, drink and be merry as there is nothing else.' Atheists and agnostics are not only found in modern times – they have existed since time immemorial. Such people are in utter darkness and misery when they get a disease or when they lose something, which they consider to be most precious. They have no one to depend on, no place to put their faith in, nothing to go back to, no solace, because whatever they think is real, is finished.

Such personalities who do not have any understanding, who do not even give a thought to the idea that there might be something other than this world, finally go to worlds of absolute darkness. That is one meaning.

The other meaning is that 'without the knowledge of the Self, one keeps wandering in the darkness of ignorance.'

They are called 'slayers of the Self.' *Ye ke cha atma hano jana* – 'Those who are slayers of the Self.' Actually, the *atman* cannot be slayed. But people, for whom the most important things in the world are those seen through their senses, who believe that there is nothing beyond their senses, are called 'slayers of the *atman*,' 'slayers of the Self.'

In another meaning, they are also 'slayers of their own Self,' because they are metaphorically killing themselves, shutting out the immortal light of the inner being and believing that they are only physical bodies. They are successfully slaying themselves! Such people go into worlds of enveloping darkness, layer upon layer of darkness. So what the *rishi* is saying is, 'Please wake up and look; there is something beyond this physical body.'

The famous sage Ramana Maharshi of Tiruvannamalai defined the whole of *Vedanta* in a nut-shell, in one sentence which he used to oft repeat – *deham naham koham soham*. This is the essence of *Vedanta*. If you know this, not just theoretically but experientially, you have known all the *Upanishads*, the entire *Vedanta*. *Deham* – 'this body,' *naham* – 'I am not.' Just as, when I am wearing clothes, you can separate me from my clothes – these are my clothes and I am different from my clothes. In the same way, *Vedanta* says, the Inner-Self is the *atman*, and the clothes that one wears is the physical body and that which belongs to me cannot be me. Therefore, I am separate and what belongs to me is separate.

So, *deham naham* – if 'I am not the body,' *koham?* – then, 'who am I?' If somebody says, 'I am just a bundle of flesh and bones,' it is fine. Let them be content with this feeling. But if somebody says, 'Let me go deeper into this matter; I may not be just a bundle of flesh and bones, I may be something different. But who am I?' Ramana Maharshi said that when one is asked this question, *koham*! 'Who am I?' *koham? Soham* is the answer – 'I am not different from That Supreme Being.' 'That Supreme Self is not different from that Supreme Being.' 'That Supreme Self am I' is similar to the *Upanishadic* statement '*tat twam asi*' – 'You are That!'

The study of the *Upanishads* is not for 'weak minds' because one has to take a totally different view of the world. The *Upanishad* itself declares, *Nayam atma balaheenay na labhya* – 'This *atman* cannot be reached by the weak.' We are not talking about physical weakness but mental weakness. It requires a great deal of mental strength to understand the *Upanishad* theoretically, and more than that to begin to live and understand it. So a great deal of strength is required and therefore it is a strength-giving message. To repeat, it is not a philosophy of running away from anything but living where you are and understanding the permanence of the Inner Reality. That is the essence of the third *shloka* – 'Those who live believing only in the permanence of this world, go to great darkness.' And they are also called *atma hano janah* – the 'slayers of the Self,' because to them, there is no immortal Self. Such people, such beings, wander around in darkness.

The fourth *shloka* describes the Supreme as immanent and transcendent which means, 'It is here, and yet It is beyond the ken of the mind and the senses'.

SHLOKA 4

anejad ekam manaso javiyo nainad deva apnuvan purvam arshat
tad dhavato nyan atyeti tishthat tasminn apo matarishva dadhati

Anejad means, 'that which does not move.' In other words, 'that Supreme Self does not move'. It is that which is unmoving.

Ekam – 'One'

Manaso javiyo – 'Even faster and swifter than the mind.' If that 'One' is faster and swifter than the mind, there is no way that the mind can find It.

Nainad deva apnuvan purvam arshat – 'There is no way that the senses can ever reach It.'

Tad dhavato nyan atyeti tishthat tasminn apo matarishva dadhati

'By itself It stands still. It out-strips those who run to reach for It. In It, the all-pervading air or energy – *prana*, supports the activities of all beings.' Now, this again seems to be one of the *Upanishadic* contradictions, because in the beginning it describes the Supreme Self, *anejad* – 'It does not move' and later, it says, 'It out-runs.'

If we go into one definition, we would have explained the others. The first one is *anejad* – 'unmoving' and the second, *manaso javiyo nainad* – 'swifter than the mind, and the senses too do not reach it, because it is ever ahead of the senses.' This is a typical attempt at describing the indescribable, which is what the *Upanishads* are all about. That *atman* or self, and Brahman or Supreme Reality, is the subject of discussion of the *Upanishads*. In the beginning of this *Upanishad*, it is said *'Ishavasyam idam sarvam'* – 'That which is everywhere, at all times.' 'That Supreme Being,' the *rishis* declare, 'is your Essential Self.' It is not a material thing that you can describe.

So, the formless, the 'attributeless,' if It can be defined at all, has to have certain 'attributes,' theoretically speaking, to help us understand. One is that 'it does not move.' This is with reference to the fact that the mind is always in movement. It is never still. It is here now, and elsewhere the next minute!

If you have read James Joyce's works, you will know what is called 'the stream of consciousness technique' where one thought is linked to another thought, and the links go on endlessly.

This unending movement is the quality of the mind-stuff, but the Supreme Reality, according to the *Upanishads*, is unmoving. Even the search for something is a movement. When one is trying to achieve something, there is the movement of trying. When the mind does not have something, it begins to look for it – so there is a movement, not in time, but in thought.

Now, the Supreme Reality which is called in the *Upanishads* as *atman*, or referred to in this *Upanishad* as *Isha*, pervades everything. Therefore, there is no question of moving from one spot to another. Movement takes place from 'here' to 'there,' but if something is everywhere, then there is no question of moving from 'here' to 'there.' It 'is.' It does not move and therefore it is different from the mind, because the mind moves. Hence one can come upon that Supreme Being, described in the *Upanishads*, when the mind has stopped all its movements, inner and outer. This is a tall order of course, but the *Upanishads*, are all about tall orders! As the *Upanishads* themselves have declared, *Nayam atma balaheenay na labhya* – 'This *atman* cannot be attained by the weak.' Strength is required.

Manaso javiyo – 'It is swifter than the mind,' which means the mind is not swift enough to reach It. Now, the mind is very swift – in a second, from 'here' it moves 'there.' But what we are talking of is always 'here,' 'there,' 'everywhere,' at the same time. Therefore the mind cannot move to It fast enough because it is there already!

The other meaning is – before the mind thinks and wants to move and reach out, *Isha*, the Supreme Being already knows about it! So, the mind cannot think faster than the Supreme Being. It also means that people who think that they can find the Truth through intellectual acrobatics, cannot find It. They deceive themselves.

Anejad ekam – 'Unmoving, swifter than the mind, the senses do not reach It, because It is ever ahead of them.' The senses, by themselves, do not reach even some physical objects. The senses, for instance, cannot reach the molecular structure or atomic structure – they need instruments. Now, here we are talking about something which is definitely beyond the reach of the senses! The senses of sight, taste, hearing, touch, smell – none of these can reach that Supreme Being. What the *rishi* is trying to say is that, attaining knowledge of the Supreme Being is not an activity of the senses. It is something else – although, from the reaction that takes place when the senses are in contact with the external world, one may draw certain conclusions that establish the existence of that Supreme Being. Since 'the senses cannot reach It' the stress is on meditation within. This is the *nivritti-marga* as opposed to *pravritti*.

The next few descriptions try to support what has already been said. 'Though it stands still, it out-strips those who run' – meaning, there is nothing which is faster than It. It is everywhere, all-pervading. It out-strips the senses; it out-strips the capacity of the mind to understand it.' Therefore, when the mind is seeking It, it cannot reach the Supreme Being. Yet 'It is still.' It has no movement. When the mind has completely stopped, when it has become absolutely still, without a single movement, then perhaps one begins to understand what the *Upanishad* is talking about.

Then it says 'Through the all-pervading *prana*, It supports the activities of beings.' It is because of the existence of this *Isha*, this Supreme Being, that there is life as we see it.

In Malayalam there is a beautiful little *bhajan* which is sung in many houses in the evening. It is significant because, unlike other bhajans, it is speculative and philosophical.

kanninu kannu, manam aakum kannu
atinu kannayidunna porul njan ennarriyum alavanandam
entu hari narayananay namah.

kanninu kannu, manam aakum kannu – 'The mind is the eye of the eye.' This is a clear and simple statement. Even if the eye is open and all the images that are in front of me are falling on my retinal screen, if my mind is not concentrated, I do not see anything. I might be thinking of something else and therefore 'seeing' something else. Therefore, 'the eye of this eye' is 'the mind' – because it is the one that sees, it observes, it decides, it chooses. The 'eye' of the physical eye is 'the mind.' 'Suppose I find out that 'I' am the 'eye' of 'the mind.' How wonderful it is! *hari narayananay namah* – this is the *kirtan.* How wonderful it is to discover that 'I' am the 'eye' of the mind, which is the eye of the eye. So, being that 'eye' of the eye, being the essence of the Consciousness, all that we see, hear, operate; everything works because of this, which is the true 'I,' which is the *atman*!

'The eye sees everything,' but the eye does not see itself. You can see your eye in a mirror as an image, but the eye does not see itself, but because it sees everything, we do not doubt its existence. Somewhat similar is the case of the *atman*. To repeat: even though the eye sees everything, it is not able to see itself. Yet it does not rule out the existence of the eye! Also, because of the eye that other objects are seen. Also, it is because of the 'I,' the consciousness, that the whole world is going on. That consciousness is absolute stillness, without any movement at all. Therefore, the closer the mind goes to this state of stillness, the more it is able to comprehend what the *Upanishad* is talking about. Of course, it is not necessary that one should be a scholar of the *Upanishads* to understand this. There are many great saints who have probably not gone through the *Upanishads*, but they say the same thing, from their experiences. Ramana Maharshi, for example, after passing through many experiences, read the scriptures and said,

'Ah, this is what I saw, this is what I felt.' He did not read first and feel later.

The fifth *shloka* is a typical presentation that sounds very close to the Zen teachings. One of the important teachings of Zen is to make it clear that even the highest level of intellect, by itself, cannot find the Supreme Truth. This is not to discourage intelligence; we are differentiating here between intelligence and intellect.

What the *Upanishad* is trying to say, what it is trying to do, is to put all our logical thinking into an arrangement that appears to be totally contradictory. That means, what we call cold logical thinking cannot be applied to the understanding of the Supreme Being. The smallest, the slightest manifestation of this understanding is what one would call 'affection' or 'love.'

If love is only given in exchange for getting something in return, like love or gifts, then that is not the love we are talking about. Love is great affection expecting nothing in return. It is rare, and there is no logic to it. Our logic is, 'My love must get me something in return.' It is logical to ask, 'Why are you giving without expecting anything in return?' This question cannot be asked to the person who really has understood how to love. He gives – you cannot ask 'For what?'

The fifth *shloka*, although it sounds as if it is another deliberate ploy to confuse, it is not. It says:

SHLOKA 5

tad ejati tan naijati tad dure tad vadantike
tad antarasya sarvasya tad u sarvasyasya baahyatah.

Tad ejati tan naijati tad dure tad vadantike – 'It moves, yet it moves not. It is far and yet it is near.'
Tad antarasya sarvasya – 'It is within all this.'
Tad u sarvasyasya baahyatah – 'It is outside all this.'

Now, on the one hand, it is a confirmation of the first *shloka* – *Ishavasyam idam sarvam* – 'That Supreme Being pervades everything here.' If it pervades everything here and if it is your essential Self, then you will understand what is meant by – 'It moves and it moves not.' It moves when we think that we are separate from it – then we move towards it. But when we understand that we are not separate from that Supreme Being, then there is no movement. Therefore, 'It moves and it moves not.'

'It is far….' If you think that it is something to be grasped, a philosophical concept or a speculative understanding, something to read and understand, then it is far. We cannot get to it because 'It is swifter than the mind.' If it is swifter than the mind, then it is very far off. Even the mind cannot reach it, leave alone the physical body.

And then the *rishi* says '…and yet it is near' which means that, when the mind has understood this implication and has absolutely quietened down and become silent, then it is near. It is seen as pervading everywhere and therefore it is here. So, 'it is far and it is near. It moves and yet it does not move.'

Tad antarasya sarvasya – 'It is within everything.'

Tad u sarvasyasya baahyatah – 'and yet it is outside.'

That means it is inside and also outside. There is no way that you can get out of this Supreme Being, whether you like it or not. Either you are within, or the Supreme Being is within you. You can look at it both ways!

Then comes the sixth *shloka*. From pure speculative philosophy so far, the *rishi* now comes to something, touching on the personal.

SHLOKA 6

yas tu sarvani bhutani atmany evaanupashyati
sarva bhuteshu chatmanam tato na vijugupsate.

He says, 'He who sees all beings in his own self, and his own self in all beings, does not feel any revulsion whatsoever.' That means, a person who begins to understand, who is absolutely still and quiet, who begins to inhale the fragrance of that Supreme Being, sees that he has no enemies anymore. He cannot be revolted he cannot be against anything or anybody, because he sees his Self in them and their Self in him. That Supreme Being pervades all. He is your *antaryami*, the *antaryami* in every one of us.

To consider yourself as a separate person, and therefore create a division between 'you' and 'me' has to cease. Only when this ceases, can we forge global unity for the human race – not through politics, not through social work, but through understanding that there is no division between 'you' and 'me.' That is the only way, because we have tried all other ways. The only way is for a human being to understand that he is not different from other human beings. That can take place only when one begins to look deep within oneself to find out what is the essential being; not what has been built around it.

That, says the *Upanishad*, is your inner *atman* which is not different from the *atman* of the other person. He who has understood that *Ishavasyam idam sarvam yat kincha jagatyam jagat* – that 'Self is the Supreme Being that pervades everything – that which moves and that which does not move; such a person has no revulsion against anybody.'

SHLOKA 7

yasmin sarvani bhutani atmaivabhud vijanatah
tatra ko mohah kah shokah ekatvam anupashyatah

This is a corollary to what has already been said before.

Yasmin sarvani bhutaniatmaivabhud vijanatah – 'When one realizes that that Supreme Self is the inner reality of all beings, when one realizes that all beings are verily his own Self,'

Tatra ko mohah kah shokah ekatvam anupashyatah- 'Such a person, who is established in complete Oneness, when he sees that all is One, where in him is the place for delusion and where is the place for sorrow?'

They say there is no cure for baldness, but there is something that is worse – jealousy. When one sees somebody prospering, one is consumed with jealousy, instead of feeling happy! Why is this? This is because one sees two people here – I am different, and you are different. But that person who sees the essential oneness of everything, enjoys another person having something. He says to himself, 'Whether I have it or that person has it, it is the same thing.' Of course, this is very easy to say but very difficult to actually feel. It needs practice to be able to feel like that, because without practice, one cannot do anything. One cannot remain in the level of theory all the time. But to practice this, one has to first firmly believe that the essential Self is not different in you and in me. 'Then there is no delusion, then there is no sorrow,' because when the world enjoys, it is my enjoyment! In the same way, therefore, such a person also must necessarily have compassion, because when somebody else suffers, it becomes his own suffering.

So, 'One who understands or is established firmly in the Oneness of the Self, has neither delusion nor sorrow.' He understands the 'oneness of the Self,' where he is 'alone' but knows that 'all is One.' Somebody once said that 'alone' really means 'all One,' although we think that 'alone' means separate.

Then comes a sort of description of the Supreme Being. If you can describe the Supreme Being at all, here is one way of describing the indescribable:

SHLOKA 8

sa paryagach chukram akaayam avranam
asnaaviram shuddham apaapa viddham
kavir manishi paribhuh svayambhur
yathatathyatorthan vyadadhac chashvatibhyas samabhyah.

Sa paryagachukram – 'He has filled all and is radiant.' That means 'He is everywhere, his radiance is everywhere' or 'That pervasive radiance is everywhere.' Here, 'radiant' is not to be misunderstood as the light which we normally know of, which is the absence of darkness. This is 'effulgence,' which is nothing to do with darkness and light. 'Spiritual effulgence' – that is what is called 'radiance.'

Akaayam – That means 'It has no body,' which means, It has no form or shape of any kind.

Avranam – 'That which is not vulnerable,' which cannot be cut or hurt or injured. 'That which cannot be injured,' not only from the physical point of view but also from the psychological point of view.

What we must understand is that, when a description of the Supreme Being is given and when it is said that one's essential identity is not different from that Supreme Being, the *yogi* who moves closer and closer to that Supreme Being begins to have these attributes little by little. So the person established in the stability of the Supreme Self also 'cannot be injured.' Of course, if he stands in the middle of the road and gets hit, he will be injured; but we don't mean that! Psychologically, one cannot injure him, because he has not made an image for himself. There is nothing that one can break, because only if one has an image can it be broken! Here, images have all been discarded and there is only stillness. Remember, as long as there is movement, there is an image.

Asnaaviram – 'He is not a physical thing,' with muscles and bones and sinew.

Shuddham – 'Pure,' absolutely pure.

Apaapa viddham – 'Untouched,' unsoiled by any kind of evil.

Kavir manishi paribhuh svayambhur yathatathyatorthan vyadadhachashvatibhyas samabhyah – 'He is the seer, the thinker, the all pervading Self.' And, since the beginning of creation, He has distributed Himself in all objects according to their own nature while remaining attributeless. The Supreme Being has divided Itself over the years into all the attributes seen in the world before us. By Itself being without any movement, It has distributed Itself into this variegated world. Therefore, to get back to It, one must turn away from this differentiation and get back into the Unity. Differentiation has taken place; now to get back into Unity is the purpose of *sadhana*.

The *Upanishad* says that 'the Supreme Being is immutable, uninjurable, absolutely still, unmoving' and so on. But what we see is the 'injurable, moving, different, divisible'; this is what we see with our senses. So it seems to be a contradiction. The *Upanishad* says that 'The Supreme Being is absolutely clear, still, silent, peaceful and all-pervading.' But we see only differences. We see only strife and chaos. The *Upanishad* teaches us to come out of this differentiation, back to the essential Unity. That is the purpose of the teaching and that is the purpose of *sadhana*.

The next *shloka*, the ninth, is very significant. It has also created a lot of confusion, because the first part of it can be easily understood, but the second part seems to be a total contradiction.

SHLOKA 9

andham tamaha pravishanti ya avidyam upasate
tato bhuya iva te tamo ya u vidyayam ratah

The first part is, *andham tamaha pravishanti ya avidyam upasate* – 'Into great darkness, blinding darkness, enter those who follow ignorance or worship ignorance.' Now this is clear. We all agree that those who worship ignorance or those who follow ignorance will enter into darkness. This is understandable.

The second part seems to be a contradiction. '*Tato bhuya iva te tamo ya u vidyayam ratah*' – but those who delight in knowledge enter into greater darkness. Now, this is a very big contradiction! Should we not learn? Does knowledge cause us to enter into greater darkness?

It is understandable that when we follow ignorance we enter into darkness. But, 'those who worship knowledge or delight in knowledge enter into greater darkness' – this is something one has to examine very carefully. The usual interpretation to this statement is that, by 'ignorance' is meant all the worldly knowledge which we have. Since it is not the knowledge of the Spirit, it is considered to be 'ignorance.' Only the understanding of Spirit is true 'knowledge.' Any knowledge which does not contribute to the understanding of the inner Self is still ignorance and therefore darkness – that is one theory.

One has to look a little more closely at the word 'knowledge.' Especially because the same *Upanishad* says, 'That Supreme Self cannot be reached by the mind or the senses.' When one says 'intelligence,' 'knowledge' and so on, it is still within the field of the mind. So one of the interpretations that can be made is this: if somebody, after studying a lot about the Supreme Being, feels he has understood the Supreme Being and is therefore rejoicing, 'he is entering into greater darkness,' because he has not understood it. He understands it only when the mind has become absolutely still and that is not the function of knowledge. The function of knowledge, the function of the intellect, the *Upanishads* say, is to lead one to understand its limitations in the field of the Spirit.

The *Upanishads* go further: 'Nothing that you worship here is the Supreme Being'! This is what the *Kena Upanishad* says:

Yan manasa na manute yenahur mano matam tadeva Brahma tvam viddhi nedam yad idam upasate – 'that which the mind cannot reach, but which is the basis of the mind, know That alone is Truth, nothing that you worship here.' When he says, 'nothing that you worship,' it does not mean that you are not supposed to do any worship. It means no activity, *pravritti*, on your part can bring about the realization of the Supreme. In fact, no *pravritti* can bring it about. It is the *nivritti marga*. Therefore, when the mind becomes quiet and when quietness enters, then 'That' is revealed.

The other point is that if one examines the actual character of what we call 'knowledge,' we come upon something very interesting. Let us say we don't have knowledge of a particular subject, and we set about trying to understand it. After some time of study, we understand it. That understanding is important. But after the understanding, what happens? When I say, 'I have knowledge of the subject' it means I have stored the understanding in my brain in the form of a memory. All knowledge is memory that has been stored, ready for retrieval. And when one says, 'I have a good memory', it means one has the capacity to retrieve correctly what has been stored at any time in the past. This is what is meant by 'having a good memory' or, in other words, 'knowledge of the subject.' Memory cannot be a thing of the present, it can only be of the past. We would not have to recall it if it is not a thing of the past. Therefore, any knowledge, including theoretical knowledge of the scriptures, lies in the past.

And what does the *Upanishad* say? *Ishavasyam idam sarvam* – 'That Supreme Being pervades everything, here and now!' So, the knowledge of the Supreme Being, is not something that can be understood, stored and kept for reference! When it is understood, it is always understood, it is always present. It is not something that can be recalled. It is not something that can be recorded and retrieved. Once there, it is always there! If it goes, then it is not the knowledge of the Supreme; because it is a memory, it has vanished. So, 'Into blinding darkness enter those who worship ignorance; into greater darkness enter those who delight in knowledge!'

Now, there is another psychological explanation to this, which is, when the mind becomes filled with the pride of having acquired knowledge and thinks that it will now see the Supreme Being, then it is very far away from understanding the Supreme, because now the ego has come in. Here, our effort should be to reverse the process and break down the barrier of ego.

Sometimes, knowledge also becomes an obstacle to the understanding of the Truth, because Truth should be absolutely clear and simple. It need not be scholastic; it need not be intellectual. And, filled with this knowledge, sometimes one does not have space in the mind to receive a glimpse of the Supreme Being, even if it comes.

There is a story about a professor who went to a great yogi and asked, 'When will I attain Self-realization?' And the yogi told him, 'Sir, you will take at least six to seven years.' Then the postman, who had come there to deliver letters to the yogi said, 'Sir, I think I must stop all this work now and keep quiet. I have this feeling of wonderful stillness coming in my heart when I come near you. I don't know what it is. Whenever I come, I listen when you talk to others – though I have not read any books…. When will I attain that absolute stillness which you talk about?' The yogi said, 'Soon, very soon; may be in a few days!'

The professor got very upset. 'What is this yogi saying? Here I am who has studied everything, and this postman knows nothing. Then how can he attain self–realization in a few days while I need six years!' When he had cooled down, the yogi said, 'Sir, it will take me six years to clear the rubbish which you have collected in your memory! When it is gone, the rest is easy!'

Then there is this famous story about the learned professor who went to the *Zen* master and said, 'I have come to understand *Zen*. Please give me *Satori* – *Zen*!' (The great experience of *Zen* is *Satori*). The master said, 'Sir, first let's have some tea.' So he made tea and then poured the tea into a cup. As he poured, the cup became full and started to overflow. The professor exclaimed, 'The cup is over-flowing!' The master turned to him and said, 'So also is your cup Sir. It is overflowing! How can I give you *Zen*? It is already full, so it is unable to receive anything. First, it has to become empty!'

The tenth *shloka* supports what has already been expressed.

SHLOKA 10

*anyad evahur vidyaya anyad ahur avidyaya
iti shushruma dhiranam ye nas tad vichachakshire.*

'They say that the result of knowledge is different from the result of ignorance. This, we have heard from the wise, who have explained it to us.' Now, the *rishi* is talking in humble terms. He does not say, 'I am saying this.' He says, 'This has been explained to me by the wise, from whom we have heard that there are two results – from knowledge comes one result and from ignorance comes another.'

This means that the process of understanding brings about a result, which is the knowledge of the object about which we seek to understand. The result of ignorance is that we do not know about the object which we are trying to understand. These are the two results. The 'object' referred to is the Supreme Self. It is not any physical or material object, but the object of enquiry of the *Upanishad* – that Supreme Being.

Knowledge and ignorance – these are the two outcomes of this process.

SHLOKA 11

vidyaam chaavidyaam cha yas tad vedobhayam saha
avidyaya mrityum tirtva vidyayaamritam ashnute.

This means, 'But one who knows these two together, knowledge and ignorance, crosses death through ignorance and attains life eternal through knowledge.'

Now, how can one cross death through ignorance and attain life eternal? 'Life eternal through knowledge,' we can understand; but how does one 'cross death through ignorance?' This is another of those difficult parts of the *Upanishad*. If we have followed what has been discussed till now, a slight glimmer of light will appear.

The *shloka* before this said that the results of knowledge and ignorance are distinct and different. This *shloka* says, 'But if you understand both, knowledge and ignorance together, then you cross death through ignorance, and life eternal through knowledge.' Now, actually, both are the same. 'Life eternal' is the same as 'crossing death.' There is no difference!

In the vedic prayer, *mrityor ma amritam gamaya* – 'lead me from *mrityu* to *amrityu*,' – it is the same thing. *Amrityu* means *amrita* – 'immortality.' That means, when one understands this concept of knowledge and ignorance which is, 'the one who worships ignorance enters into darkness and the one who worships knowledge enters into greater darkness,' then one has understood knowledge and ignorance together for what they really stand. If you have understood that, then you have 'crossed death and attained life eternal.'

'Crossed death through ignorance' – there must be some reason why they have used 'ignorance' with 'death' and put them together. 'Understanding ignorance' means 'to be free of that ignorance.' You cannot be free of something until you have understood it. If you want to be free of violence, you have to first understand what violence is, in all its intricate patterns, and this cannot be done by sitting for years in a cave. It has to be done only in society. There is nobody to be violent with in the cave. Only when you come out of the cave, interact with others and get hurt in the process, will you really know whether or not you are really free of anger and violence.

So, to understand ignorance means to understand the implications of the meaning of ignorance. And when you have understood that, you are free of death. When you have understood that the Supreme Being which pervades everything, which pervades the entire universe, is no different from your Self, then there is no death for you.

Even a yogi or a *rishi* who has understood or has taught the *Upanishad* dies physically. Physical death is there for everyone. But the yogi understands that his inner Self does not die. Therefore, he 'crosses over death.' *Amrita* does not mean 'to be free from physical death'; it means, 'to understand that the inner Self or the inner Consciousness does not cease to exist with the demise of the physical body.'

The twelfth *shloka* is about the manifest world and the unmanifest cause–the manifest and the unmanifest Brahman.

SHLOKA 12

andham tamah pravishanti ye asambhutim upasate
tato bhuya iva te tamo ya u sambhutyam rataah.

'Into blinding darkness enter those who worship the unmanifest and into still greater darkness, as it were, enter those who delight in the manifest!' The same style of teaching occurs again and again in the *Upanishad*.

Now, the 'manifest' means 'the world' that is 'manifested' – the world that we see in everyday life. Let us start from the last part of this *shloka* – 'they enter greater darkness who delight in the manifest.' That means, those who delight only in the physical world and whose relationship with the world is only physical, going nothing beyond food, drink, sleep and sex – 'they enter into greater darkness'. This is very simple. Unless we have chosen not to look, we see the darkness. That means, at every step there is a problem and at every step there is the spectre of sorrow and death haunting us. This is not being pessimistic; this is fact. Everything is indeterminate, unknown. We never know when life is going to end. We do not know when something will last, and when something will end. We never know when the little snatches of happiness that we have, are going to escape from our hands. As one progresses, as one grows older and older, one begins to see that life is coming slowly to a close. Going nearer and nearer to the end, one begins to see that one is staring into darkness – there is nothing to see, there is nothing to gain, nothing to get, nothing more to enjoy.

There are those who worship the unmanifest. They also enter into darkness, but not as great a darkness as those who worship only the manifest. 'Worshipping the unmanifest' means worshipping that which is the cause of the manifest world. The *Upanishadic* teaching is that one has to transcend both, the manifest and the unmanifest. When they speak of the unmanifest they are speaking about the Supreme Reality as a creator, destroyer and so on. It is

29

unmanifest because it is behind the manifestations that we see before us. It is the operator of all that operates. The *Upanishad* says that you can remain at that level, but the Truth, which is Light, is beyond both, the manifest as well as the unmanifest. That means we have to transcend even the very differentiation between the individual self and the Supreme Being. The manifest is the individual and the unmanifest is the Supreme. One has to understand that the individual self and the Supreme Being are one and the same. Otherwise, according to the *Upanishad*, we are still operating, comparatively, from a level of darkness.

Since we are dealing with *Upanishadic* philosophy we are dealing with death as in the 'death' of the 'conditioned individual,' and the manifestation of the immeasurable Supreme Being. Therefore, we chant the last shlokas of the Upanishad, the funeral prayers, in the end so that the 'little I' is cremated and the 'larger I,' *Ishwara* or *Isha*, manifests itself. There are several initiation rites in many mystic orders that celebrate the 'death' of the initiate. When the 'little ego,' the 'little I' is done with and becomes still, then the 'greater I' manifests itself. This is the message of the *Upanishad*.

Swami Vivekananda once summed up the essence of the whole of the Hindu religion and culture by saying, 'Man is essentially divine. To manifest this divinity through work, worship, meditation or knowledge is the sum and substance of the Hindu religion, the Hindu teaching.' All other things are just incidental.

So far, we have in detail gone into the genesis of what *Upanishad* means and what the *Ishavasya Upanishad* says. Starting with the first *shloka*, we have come up to the twelfth *shloka*.

It is desirable to recount in a nutshell what we have gone through and then return to the next.

The *Upanishad*, in its essence, is a teaching given from a teacher, personally, to a learner or a student. It is not a text that is to be treated merely at a scholastic level. It is to do with the inner awakening, and that is one of the reasons why the *Upanishads* were reserved for those who had already gone through everything else in life and come to the last stage. The ancients divided the different stages of life into the four *ashramas* – *brahmacharya, grihasta, vanaprasta* and *sanyasa*. The study of the *Upanishads* was partly taken up during *brahmacharya*, but the most important aspects were generally taken up during the *vanaprasta* stage, expect in notable exceptions where the student, as a *brahmachari*, had the capacity to go directly to the *Upanishad*, which is a very important and advanced part of the *Vedas*. That is why the *Upanishad* is also called *Vedanta* – it comes at the end of the other portions of the *Vedas*. After one mastered the *Samhitas* and the *Brahmanas*, one went to the *Aranyakas* and the *Upanishads*. *Aranyaka* means 'forest' and therefore the Upanishads are sometimes referred to as 'forest-scriptures' which were taught in forest-hermitages.

Therefore, it is not merely a study to compare and criticize, or for intellectual hair-splitting. It is more to do with one's inner development. It is a guide, a blueprint to the inner development. This is the spirit with which the *Upanishad* has to be studied. The word '*Upanishad*' itself means that.

As explained, *upa* means 'to go closer,' 'to go nearer.' *Shad* means 'to sit and listen'; and '*ni*' indicates the student's humility in admitting that he is at a lower level than the teacher. Even the teacher speaks with great humility when he says, 'This is what we have heard, as taught by the ancients.'

The *Ishavasya Upanishad* is part of the *Yajur Veda*. The first *shloka* is actually the sum and substance of the entire *Upanishad*. If we go deep into the first and the second *shlokas*, we actually have the whole *Upanishad*. The first *shloka* is '*Ishavasyam idam sarvam yat kincha jagatyam jagat tena tyaktena bhunjitha ma gridah kasya svid dhanam*'.

Ishavasyam idam sarvam – 'that Supreme Being pervades everything here.' *Yat kincha jagatyam jagat* – 'that which moves and that which does not move.' *Tena tyaktena bhunjitha* – 'therefore, give up and rejoice!' Now, this is the key phrase of the *Upanishad*

– 'give up' or 'let go.' Normally, when we say 'enjoy' or 'rejoice' we mean 'acquire and rejoice!' Here is an *Upanishad* which says 'give up and rejoice!' So 'give up' not only means 'to give up physical objects' it also means, 'to let go of the mind's hold on the ego.' That is more important. When you 'let go,' then the mind is cleared and one experiences, or at least, one goes close to the understanding of '*Ishavasyam idam sarvam*' – 'that Supreme Being pervades everything here.' And, says the Upanishad, 'The one who begins to understand this can live a hundred years doing his *karmas* without fear of getting even one blot on his life from the effects of his *karmas*.'

The second *shloka* says '*Jijivishet shatam samah*' – for one hundred years one can work, '*na karma lipyate nare*' – *karma* does not touch you. When one begins to understand what has been said in the first *shloka*, then from there, the *Upanishadic* thought is developed and brought to the understanding of:
- what is real and what is unreal;
- what is knowledge and what is ignorance;
- how knowledge alone cannot lead to understanding the Supreme Being;
- that the highest understanding that should come out of knowledge is to understand the limitations of that intellectual knowledge;
- that it is not the intellect that is more important but some other quality which helps the clearing of the inner-centres so that the energies of the Supreme Being are free to act without obstacles.

Then the *Upanishad* explains the condition of such a person who has understood this concept of the Supreme Being pervading everywhere, the Supreme Being being as his very own Self, and therefore also the very Self of all other beings. For such a person, the *Upanishad* asks, 'Where can there be sorrow and how can there be death, for he has understood that everything is himself!'

For a person who has understood that his inner spirit is the same as the inner spirit in the other person, 'Where is delusion? Where is sorrow? Where is death?' Physical death is common to all. So when they say, *amrita* – 'immortality,' it does not mean that one will remain alive forever. It means that the person realizes that the inner essence does not end with the end of the physical body. It remains forever in its own essential bliss.

Then we came to the examination of what is knowledge and what is ignorance. Here the statement is made, 'He who worships ignorance enters into darkness and he who worships knowledge, who delights in knowledge alone, enters into greater darkness.' We examined this carefully and discussed why this statement is made; mere intellectual knowledge cannot take one to the Supreme Being and no verbal acrobatics can ever lead one to self-realization.

We also discussed the level upto which the intellect and the mind can travel, after which the mind in its subtlety, in the height of its awareness, understands the limitations of mere cerebration and then quietens down. In that stillness comes about the realization of the Supreme Being. Great intellectual giants who have been in the forefront of *Vedantic* thought, especially Adi Shankaracharya (who wrote so many commentaries on the *shastras*), were also aware of the fact that there is a level beyond which the mind cannot travel.

Now we come to the thirteenth *shloka*, where distinction is made between what is manifest and what is unmanifest.

SHLOKA 13

anyad evahuh sambhavad anyad ahur asambhavat
iti shushruma dhiranam ye nas tad vichachakshire.

Anyad evahuh sambhavad anyad ahur asambhavat – 'Indeed, they say, the results of the manifest are distinct from the results of the unmanifest.'

Iti shushruma dhiranam ye nas tad vichachakshire – 'Thus we have heard from the ancients, the results that come from the worship of the manifest are different from the results of worshipping the unmanifest.'

The difference between the manifest and the unmanifest is that 'manifest' means 'the world which is manifested out of the Supreme Being,' and 'the unmanifest' is 'the cause of this manifestation.' So the results of worshipping the two are different. The unmanifest is that Supreme Being from whom this manifestation has taken place. One who worships the unmanifest, who tries to understand the inner core of this manifest world, realizes ultimately that the core is his own inner Self and therefore the inner self of all living beings.

The one who worships the manifest world often completely ignores the source and cause – the unmanifest Supreme Being – and believes that the manifest world is all that 'is.' His values are entirely based on the manifest and therefore when sorrow strikes him, or when death overtakes him, everything is at an end.

When we come face to face with disease and death, then we begin to understand the foolishness of depending only on the manifest, because soon it is all going to disappear, and we wonder 'Is there something permanent other than this?' That question is what the *Upanishads* ask and try to answer, or rather, try to bring out the answer from us. Dialogue is a very important method of teaching in the *Upanishads*. If one imposes an answer on somebody, then that is a second-hand answer and after sometime it will be forgotten or ignored. The answer has to come from within. Therefore it is more important to keep a question alive than to get a ready-made answer from somebody. And it all depends on our personal *sadhana* because, as we keep the question in mind and do our *sadhana*, the psychic capacity, or let us say, the 'intellectual' capacity to answer this question also increases. Then we discover that our answer is where our question started.

Introspection is something that one should not avoid and has to do. One should not look for ready-made answers. There are ready-made answers available in books, but they mean nothing unless they form part of our own experience. And the strength of the *Upanishads* lies in taking us on to this experience within. That is why sometimes they go through these subtle intellectual acrobatics, so that the answer is worked out within oneself.

So, for those who worship only the manifest world, the result is different from the result of the worship of the unmanifest, which is the cause of this manifest world. But sometimes pure introspection can go to extremes. The *Ishavasya Upanishad* is one of the *Upanishads* that tries to bring about a balance between too much monasticism and too much worldliness. That is why the second *shloka* says, 'Do your *karma* for a hundred years; don't run away! If you do it with the understanding that the Supreme Being pervades everything, then the effect of the *karma* will not touch you.' This is one of the principal *Upanishads*, and also one of the oldest, which tries to bring about a balance between extreme monastic life on one side, and worldly life on the other.

After explaining that the result of worshipping the unmanifest is different from the effect of worshipping the manifest, the next *shloka* says:

SHLOKA 14

sambhutim cha vinasham cha yas tad vedobhayam saha
vinashena mrityum tirtva sambhutya amritam ashnute.

'He who understands the manifest and the unmanifest together, crosses death.' This is said because one could otherwise become one-sided and forget the world and concentrate only on the unmanifest! This is almost impossible because it requires a great deal of physical, mental, and psychological preparation. 'Understanding the unmanifest and the manifest together' means to live where you are, and simultaneously go on with your studies and your search for the Truth, giving enough importance to the manifest as well as the unmanifest, until you begin to understand the truth that the Supreme Being is the only living reality, and is all-pervading. Only then can you give up the manifest, but not before that, because it is a question of maturity. Few human beings reach that level of maturity where they can directly go to the unmanifest, giving no attention to the manifest. But, if the rest, who are not ready, try to imitate them, they might go some distance but come back again. *Vairagya* is important, but *vairagya* should not be like what Sri Ramakrishna Paramahamsa used to call 'the monkey's *vairagya*!'

So, one has to go carefully. Keep the manifest in view, keep the unmanifest in view, balance the two and move forward. When one is completely convinced, then one can drop the manifest. In fact, you do not even have to drop it. *Maya* pushes you out; you don't have to even try! For example: When the embryo is in the womb of the mother for nine months, the muscles of the womb protect the embryo until it matures. When it is matured and has become a child who is ready to emerge, then the same muscles that were protecting the embryo, push the child out because the child has attained the level of maturity to be free.

When maturity develops by study, understanding, *sadhana*, meditation and other means, then automatically you are out of the manifest, you don't have to try to come out! The moment you try to come out half-heartedly it means there is much more distance left to travel. When the understanding comes, it comes at once, nothing can stop it! When the understanding comes, one does not have this uncertainty whether one should give up or not. As long as uncertainty is there, stick to what you have and carry on slowly; do your *sadhana*, study, be at peace.

In Shirdi, there are two words written on top of the *samadhi* of Shirdi Sai Baba: *Shraddha* and *Saburi*. In Marathi, *saburi* means 'patience,' like *sabar* in Hindi. This patience is of great importance, even in *sadhana*. People become very impatient – 'I've been doing this *bandha*, that *bandha*, this *yoga* and that meditation – and the *kundalini* is still not rising within me!' This is the complaint one hears often. But you see, first of all, your mind is so agitated! Cool it down, calm it down; let us be patient. One works a lifetime to build up a decent bank balance. But when it comes to *sadhana*, everything has to be done in a week's time. Otherwise it is not worth it! For everything else we don't mind working and slaving for years, but for this search, magical solutions are expected! Unfortunately, there are some who say that they can provide this magic through short-cuts. That is another problem.

The *shlokas* from the fifteenth upto the eighteenth are chanted at the funeral rites.

SHLOKA 15

hiranmayena patrena satyasyaapihitam mukham
tattwam pushann apaavrinu satya dharmaya drishtaye.

Hiranmayena paatrena satyasyaapihitam mukham: 'The face of the Supreme Truth is covered by a golden disc.' And the student says, 'O *Pushann*, O *Surya*, O controller of everything, remove this golden disc that covers your face, so that I, who love the Truth, may perceive It!' This is a beautiful prayer. This prayer is only for the one who loves the Truth, who prays, 'May I see it in all its glory.'

This 'golden disc' that covers the face of Truth is the captivating glamour and glitter of the world. Often, most of us are carried away by the shining 'golden disc.' So this prayer is, 'I can do nothing about this golden-disc except plead; please remove it O *Pushann*, O Controller, so that I may see you as you are, as the Real Truth!'

Since *Pushann* also means *Surya*, the Sun-God, the 'golden disc' could also figuratively refer to the golden color of the sun when it rises in the morning and sets in the evening. 'Remove that golden disc so that I may see your face.' It also means, 'Remove all the attributes so that I may see you as the Attributeless Supreme Being.' This is the second interpretation.

The second part of this prayer, which is, 'I, who am the lover of Truth,' is important. If one is not the lover of 'Truth' then one can be happy with that golden disc alone. One does not want to look beyond it.

Now, even after going through this *Upanishad*, the student has to still make a prayer and say, 'Please remove this golden disc so that I may see you face-to-face.' It is noteworthy that even at the highest level of intellectual speculation, prayer still has importance. If you say, 'I am the Supreme Being, so I don't have to pray' then you don't have to, provided you really know. Otherwise, prayer is important till one has crossed that distinction. And prayer is not a 'silly thing' which has come down to us from ancient times as a leftover item from the primitive people who worshipped fire and the elements. It has been seen that through prayer, even disease and physical problems can be cured to a great extent. If a hundred people pray together, if their minds are fixed together on attaining an objective, there are more chances of getting it than when one single person is trying to do the same. When we go to a holy place where thousands of pilgrims have come and prayed, there is a certain change that takes place in us. It is partly because of the atmosphere of the place, and the major contribution to the atmosphere are the thousands of people who go there, with their minds fixed on the Deity. The mental energy of millions of people gets accumulated at that holy place and so when we go there, we share it.

The *Upanishad* is trying to say that ultimately, the most important truth is within. When a temple is built, and the image of the deity is actually being made, the sculptor sits on the chest and knocks at the nose, because it has not yet become the Deity – it is still a stone. And then when the image is complete, there begins an elaborate process. The *vedic kriya* called *prana pratishta* is done, then the *homa* – the holy fire is lit, then the *avahan*, and so on. The person who does the *prana pratishta* first clears up his own inner-heart – *hridaya*. Then he does the *avahan* – he invites the Deity to come and settle in his heart, his temple within, and from there he transfers the energy to the heart of the stone deity in the actual temple and the *prana pratishta* has been completed. That Deity has become God! So it is from within, within the heart, that the whole thing starts.

So 'I, who love to see the 'Truth' request you, pray to you, please remove this golden disc that covers your countenance, so that I may come face to face with you as the Supreme Truth' – is the first prayer.

SHLOKA 16

pushann ekarshe yama surya prajapatya vyuha
rashmin samuha tejah
yat te rupam kalyanatamam tat te pashyami yo saav asau
purushah so ham asmi.

Pushann ekarshe yama surya prajapatya vyuha rashmin samuha tejah – these are all descriptions of *Surya* or *Pushann;* the Controller, the Seer, the off-spring of *Prajapathi*.

Yat te rupam kalyanatamam tat te pashyami yo saavasau purushah so ham asmi – 'Spread forth your rays – gather up your Light so that I may behold you.' Let us say that the golden-disc has been removed and the 'Truth' shines forth in all its glory. Then the disciple says, 'Please gather up your rays; let me behold you because the flash is too much for the physical eyes, for me, the limited being, to see you. Please then show me your radiant form so that I can come to terms with what I am seeing.'

If we go into the Old Testament, there is something similar given there. When Moses went up the Mount, he is supposed to have seen God in the form of a 'burning bush' – Light. He sees nothing but a light shining. The story is that Moses did not see the bare Truth. The brightness would have blinded him. So it was seen from behind the tree which looked like a 'burning bush.' And when Moses entered wearing his shoes, a voice said, 'Remove your shoes, for you are on sacred land!' This is what we do when we go to a temple – we remove our shoes and enter.

Again we draw a parallel between the *Upanishad* and the Old Testament. Moses asked this Light that was burning behind the tree, 'Who are you?' because at that time, he probably thought that God was somebody sitting in heaven with a crown on his head. The answer he got in the Hebrew language was – *ahiyae ashar ahiyae* – which means 'I am That I am!' There is no other way that it can be described but as 'I am That I am!'

So here, after praying for the golden disc to be removed the devotee says, 'Please gather up your radiant light so that I may see your lovely form.' The word 'form' is being used because, for most people, a form is necessary to relate to. To understand and have a relationship with an attributeless nothingness is next to impossible for most people. This is why the system of worship through images has been established.

You may choose the image you are comfortable with – the divine mother, or *Krishna*, or the *Siva Linga*. 'Please show me your beautiful form so that I may rejoice in it!'

From the form, one can go to the formless. Lest people mistake the meaning of the prayer and think that it talks about wanting to see the Supreme Being in form alone, the *rishi* adds, 'That *purusha* who I want to see, that am I!' *Soham Asmi*! 'That which I seek to see, to whom I pray, is no different from my Inner Self.' This is a beautiful prayer. It not only asks the Supreme to be seen, it also says, 'That Essence, that great Being whom I, the lover of 'Truth' would like to see in Its wondrous form – *Soham Asmi*! That is not different from my own 'Inner Being,' my own Inner Essence!' That means, I exist because of It; if That is not, then I am not.

Now, while this is the teaching in the *Upanishad*, which is a highly speculative and philosophical text, the *bhakta* in his simplicity, comes to the same point! The *Vedantin*, after going through the *Vedantic* texts and meditating on it, comes to the understanding that the Supreme Being transcends the limitations of the intellect. The *bhakta*, however from the beginning says, 'I know nothing except that I can't find 'Him' through the intellect, so let me attach my mind to that Supreme Being. The *Vedas* have said it, so let me have faith and fix my mind.'

In the case of *Bhakti*, it begins with faith; in the case of *Jnana* or intellectual reasoning it begins with doubt; but in the end, the conclusion is that realization comes about when the mind has become absolutely still, either through *bhakti* or through *karma* or through *jnana* or through *Vedanta*. As long as this 'little I' is super-active, 'the real I' will not manifest itself. When 'this' becomes quiet and silent, then 'That' manifests itself as one's own Supreme Self. This is the teaching of the *Upanishad*.

There is a very interesting book called *Bardo – The Tibetan Book of the Dead*. When a person is about to die and he is on his deathbed, the chief lama goes and sits near the person, holds his hand and chants the 'Bardo' in Tibetan. If you translate it into Sanskrit it will sound just like the seventeenth *shloka*:

SHLOKA 17

vayur anilam amritam athedam bhasmantam shariram
aum krito smara kritam smara krito smara kritam smara.

Vayur anilam amritam athedam:
'May this life enter into the immortal breath' – this is the prayer. This is still chanted when a person dies. Perhaps it was originally intended that one sits and chants this when a person is dying, is going away. The mind is reminded that this life, the soul, is entering into the Immortal Breath.

Bhasmantam shariram – 'This body is becoming ashes.' The person is reminded, 'You are not the body! The body is ending in ashes, but you are going to the other sphere, mingling with the Vital Breath.'

And then, a message to the intelligence; '*Aum krito smara kritam smara krito smara kritam smara*' – 'Remember, remember what we are doing here; remember what we are telling you, remember O Intelligence, remember!' 'Go! Go with this understanding; remember that you are the Supreme Spirit; remember that your body is becoming ashes and you are free! Mingling with the immortal breath, go!'

Aum krito smara kritam smara krito smara kritam smara.

This is a prayer chanted when a person is dying. Now we come to the question: Is it to be obtained only when a person is dying? Or is it something which we should remember at all times? Because, who knows when death comes? So let us say that death is like a welcome friend – always with us! Even if you are afraid of it, it won't go away. So why be afraid of it? Stay with it! Death is ever at our doorstep. It is our companion. It is nothing to worry about. Therefore remember; let this life mingle with the vital breath. That Supreme Being am I – *Soham Asmi*. It is a reminder, not merely a ritual.

Now again, when we speak of death, is man really afraid of death? Or is a human being afraid of losing his possessions? We know nothing about death, really speaking. If somebody were to guarantee you that whatever you had you could take with you when you die, then would you be afraid of death? It is the fear that whatever we hold near and dear to us, will be left behind.

There is a famous story of Guru Nanak. When Guru Nanak was wandering around he met a Nawab Saheb who was a big miser, who would not part with a single penny. Guru Nanak was always helping people. Wherever he went, he opened what are called 'langars' which operate even today in all Gurudwaras. Any person going to a Gurudwara can get free food and accommodation for a few days.

Guru Nanak wanted to teach a lesson to the Nawab Saheb. One day he took a sewing needle, wrapped it up, wrote a note and sent it to the Nawab. The note said, 'Nawab Saheb, I pay my respects to you. I am sending you a sewing needle. Please keep it safe with you. I feel that you and I will pass away very soon. So when we meet in the other world, please return this sewing needle to me! It is a small help you can do for me. Please keep it safe until then!'

The Nawab got quite perturbed. Deep down in his heart he respected Guru Nanak, and felt that perhaps what the holy man said about death might come true, and if he gave a promise to a saint, he would have to keep it. So he replied, 'Sir you have put me in a fix! How am I going to carry this sewing needle after my death and give it back to you? Sorry, I cannot take this needle.' Then Guru Nanak said, 'In that case, how do you expect to take all your money with you? Why don't you give to the needy?'

When the human being comes to understand that at some moment or the other all his worldly activity will cease, and he says to himself, 'Let me think that all this has already ceased. Then how would I lead my life? What would I clear up so as to live like that?' He will then live accordingly.

Do you know how the *Bhagavat* was written? King Parikshit was told that he was going to die in seven days. So he decided, 'Now that I am going to die, let me do something worthwhile.'

If you look at this matter carefully, every night we die in a way, and come alive in the morning. Can we not say that every minute we are dying, because what has already happened to us is gone forever? Psychologically, it is possible to think that we are dead to what happened to us yesterday. You twisted my ear yesterday. I carry the memory for twenty years, wanting to twist your ear back! The actual event is finished, but I have been carrying it with me and nursing it carefully for years. Can one die to this kind of situation? Swami Vivekananda once said, 'Yesterday is dead, forget it! Tomorrow has not come, don't worry! Today is here, use it!' '*Aum krito smara kritam smara krito smara kritam smara* – 'Remember, Remember, Remember.' And the last *shloka* is:

SHLOKA 18

agne naya supatha raye asmaan vishvaani deva
vayunaani vidvaan
yuyodhya asmaj juharaanam eno bhuyisthaam te nama
uktim vidhema.

This is addressed to the God of fire, *Agni. Agni* was always considered to be a powerful deity because fire has the capacity to burn everything to ashes and equalize them.

'Sceptre and crown must tumble down
And in the dust be equal made.'

Fire has always been a symbol of the spirit. In ancient times, when the matchstick was not invented, fire had to be lit by rubbing dry flint to dry firewood, and the fire came from a spark. And the question asked was, 'Where was this fire before it came out?' So, it was used as a symbol for the inner Self that manifests itself and then goes back into the unmanifest.

You will also notice that with one candle you can light a hundred candles without diminishing the flame. That again is a reason why *Agni* is given so much importance because, from one *atman* can be 'lit' several *atma*, and yet nothing is reduced here! *Purnamadah purnamidam purnaat purnamudachyate purnasya purnamaadaaya purnamevaavashishyate.'*

Again, fire gives light. In ancient times there was no electricity and we had to light a lamp to see the face of the deity in the *garbha griha*, in the temple.

To that *Agni* one prays, 'Lead us along the auspicious path to prosperity…. Prosperity, not only in this world but also after death. *Agni*, you who know what we are doing; we admit to you what we are doing – right and wrong. You, who are the knower of everything, lead us unto prosperity. Take away all sins from us. Take away all deceitfulness from us. Burn it to ashes and we shall offer many prayers unto you forever! We shall continue to burn all our

bad *karma* in You, O *Agni*! Destroy our bad karma, turn all our bad deeds to ashes and lead us to the path of prosperity.'
This is how the *Ishavasya Upanishad* ends.

Om Shantih! Om Shantih! Om Shantih!

QUESTIONS AND ANSWERS

Q: *'In the* Upanishad, *there is a passage requesting the Sun, the originator, to remove the shield which covers Him. My question is, can a person get self-enlightenment without going into* samadhi? *Is the shield removed only with* samadhi?'
A: This may sound like a technical question, but actually it is something that a sincere *sadhak* would like to understand. *Samadhi* has been interpreted in different ways. Some people think that *samadhi* is always a trance-state. Others think *samadhi* is a state of natural being where there is no trance.

The question is, 'Can a person get self-enlightenment without going into *samadhi*' or, is the 'removing of the shield' to do only with *samadhi*?

The word *samadhi*, which is very frequently used in *sadhana*, occurs in the *Ashtanga Yoga Sutras* of Patanjali. There, it is actually split into three different parts. The words used there are *dharana, dhyana, samadhi*.

Dharana means fixing your attention completely, to the exclusion of everything else, on the object, idea or image that is foremost in your mind at that moment. Suppose you want to meditate on the Supreme Reality as having a form, you fix your complete attention on That. If you want to fix your attention on Om as an abstract symbol of the Supreme Reality, then to have your complete attention on That, to the exclusion of any other thought, is *dharana*.

Dhyana is when this continues uninterruptedly for a length of time, without any conflict or confusion. Continuous *dharana* is *dhyana*.

Samadhi is the culmination of *dharana* and *dhyana*. It is the state in which one is so absorbed in the object or idea that one is meditating upon, that the separateness between that and the individual who is meditating is dissolved. This is called *samadhi*, where only that which is meditated upon remains, and everything else has subsided. The individual no longer exists, at least for the time.

If *samadhi* means this, then it is definitely necessary to go into *samadhi* or to experience *samadhi* to get the 'cover' removed. Even if it is a form of trance in which the individual ego is not completely erased, that is also a kind of *samadhi*. There are different forms of *samadhi* – *nirvikalpa, vikalpa, savikalpa* – these are all different states of consciousness described in yogic terms, to represent a certain stage of a person's development.

But the *samadhi* which is necessary for the Ultimate Supreme Truth to reveal itself is the *samadhi* where the individual consciousness has been erased, the ego has been erased, and what remains is the Supreme Being. Therefore, it is necessary to go into *samadhi* for 'self-realization,' the understanding of the Supreme Being, not just a *devata* or an image.

Q: *Can you make a comparison and contrast between* vidya-avidya; sambhuti-asambhuti? *And what is* atma hanojanah – *who are called the 'slayers of* Atman' *which is expressed in the* Upanishad?
A: First, *vidya* and *avidya*. When you add 'a' before a word it negates it. So *avidya* means that which is not knowledge – 'ignorance.' Any *vidya* that is not directly connected to the understanding of the Supreme Being is automatically classified as *avidya*. From the point of view of the Upanishad, *vidya* is only that which takes one to the understanding of the Supreme Brahman. Any other *vidya* may be called *vidya*, in the ordinary

sense of the term, but from the point of view of the *Upanishad*, it is still *avidya*, because it is still in the relative world of ignorance. So, this distinction has to be made. What you call *vidya* need not be *vidya* in the *Vedantic* sense of the term; it may be classified as *avidya*.

Regarding *sambhuti* and *asambhuti* – the manifest and the unmanifest – the manifest means the differentiation that we see with our five senses and the mind. We see that things are separate. This is the manifest. When the *sadhak* has reached a state of total unity in himself, the same manifest has ceased to exist for him and only the unmanifest exists. So it depends on the understanding and experience of the *sadhak* whether he divides things into the manifest, or considers everything as the unmanifest. From the absolute standpoint there is no division between the manifest and the unmanifest. The unmanifest-manifest division comes only when viewed through the limited understanding of the human mind.

Atma hanojanah – 'the slayers of the *atman*' – means those who consciously avoid understanding, avoid even the attempt to understand the Inner Being, those who believe and live with the feeling that it is only the body and the outside world that is real. Such persons are called ' *Slayers* of the *atman*' – *atma hanojanah*.

Q: *When physical death happens, does the mind leave along with the soul? Does 'mind' mean the vasanas that are acquired? Is death the end of everything or is there something that survives forever?*
A: One can go into this topic theoretically. One will say that it ends with the body, while another will say that the soul survives forever. But this would be merely theoretical. We can often prove one side or the other, and the debate could go on endlessly.

But from the point of view of those who have performed *sadhana* and have experienced the 'Self' for such beings who have understood, and are completely convinced that the 'Self' is other than the body, 'something' continues. It does not cease with the cessation of the physical body. How it continues, where it continues, whether it carries *vasanas* with it – these are subsidiary questions. The basic fact is that when the body is finished, the consciousness survives. For the person with self-realization, the consciousness that survives is already linked with the Supreme Consciousness. Therefore, he is not even concerned whether It exists as an individual or as a universal reality. That is why the study of the *Upanishad* is not merely a theoretical study or a theoretical discussion. It is more to do with inner understanding.

As one progresses internally, one also continues with *nidhidhyasana*, with the understanding, with the study, so that both develop equally. And then at one point, a person is able to internalize and understand what he has till that time been verbally understanding. So this is an internal exercise, rather than external.

Q: *Is* Upanishad *closer to* dvaita *philosophy?*
A: This is a scholarly question requiring a bit of explanation. There is a general tendency, especially among Western Orientalists, to think that *Vedanta* means only *Advaita vedanta* of Shankara. This is not true. From Adi Shankaracharya onwards, right upto Madhva, Vallabhacharya and Ramanujacharya, different views of *Vedanta* have been expressed. Now to the question: 'Is the *Upanishad* closer to *dvaita* philosophy?' Well, the great acharyas who have written these commentaries expressing different views about *dvaita, advaita, vishishta advaita* and so on, certainly did not write it to confuse people! If there is any confusion, it is due to our misunderstanding of the factual position. Without doubt, they all had some experience of the Supreme Being. They did not merely read existing books and write explanatory notes! Therefore, if there is some misunderstanding and division between these views of thought, these divisions have to be removed by people who are ready to shed their differences, sit together and sort it out. Otherwise we will always remain split.

No teacher, none of the *acharyas*, have questioned the basic te-
net of *Vedanta*, which is that essentially the human is divine, and
that the *atman* which survives the physical body is the Inner Essence. Everybody admits this. Also, everybody admits that *sadhana*,
which includes the purifying of the mind through leading a disci-
plined life, is necessary. All *acharyas* have said that, the less you are
caught up in the vagaries of the senses, the easier it is to go nearer
to the Supreme Being. So, if these basic tenets are accepted, you
need not worry about which philosophy to follow! All *acharyas* are
unanimous on this matter.

There have been other differences. Someone says that the Supreme Being and the *atman* are not different; that the *jivatma* is
only an imaginary division from the Supreme Being; that there is
only the *Brahman* and nothing else.

A second view is that the *jiva* is different from the *atman* but it
may merge and partake of the glories of the *Paramatman*.

The third view is that the *jiva* will always remain separate and
subservient to the Supreme Reality.

But even they who preach *dvaita* have not questioned the fact
that the *sadhak* has to lead a pure life, has to purify his mind, has to
meditate, has to go deep within himself so that he realizes his inner
atman which is called the *antaryami*.

And so, instead of going into the theoretical discussion whether
this path is right or that path is right, one should take up the
common factor which all the *acharyas* have stressed upon: purify
yourself, do your *sadhana*, go deeper into yourself, find out the
'inner self,' and then decide which *acharya* is to be followed. This is
the right path, instead of simply staying on the theoretical ground
and having a difference of opinion.

There is one other thing which we can understand here. Suppose I am a great *bhakta* of Krishna and I begin with *bhajans* and
kirtans, and go closer to Krishna. Now, in a high stage of devotion,
when my mind is completely absorbed in the glories of Krishna,
when the only thought in the mind is of Krishna, when the whole

world has melted – the psychological, inner aspect, not the physical reality – when the whole world has melted and all that I know is Krishna; I speak Krishna, I eat, drink and sleep Krishna, everything is Krishna, then where is the question of 'I?' I don't exist. Only Krishna exists!

Or, if one substitutes the word 'Krishna' with *Brahman*, only *Brahman* exists.

So in answer to this question, one should for the time being leave aside the external, theoretical understanding. If one feels inclined to follow the *dvaita* doctrine, well and good. But keep in mind that what is necessary is a pure life, purification, *sadhana* and whatever contributes to this *sadhana* – meditation, kirtan, puja, japa or anything else. The whole process of *sadhana* is to purify the mind so that it becomes absolutely clear. When it is clear, then it is left for one to decide whether the bliss one feels is because the *atman* is the Supreme Being, or whether it is a 'reflection of the glory' of the Supreme Being – the *atma bhava* as they call it in *dvaita*. That need not confuse us now. Let us try to find the 'Inner Self' first.

Q: *Temper is my main problem. If I do sadhana I am able to improve. But then my approach to the mundane world becomes indifferent. I am not able to lead a normal life, enjoying the worldly attributes. Is this common?*

A: Temper is a common problem. So you need not think that you are isolated on this issue. Many people have the problem of quick temper or bad temper. Some may bottle it up; others may express it, but it is there. One is able to improve this with meditation but that makes one indifferent to the mundane world! This is a genuine problem. It is not common, but it is so, especially when people are *sadhaks*. For those who are not *sadhaks*, who are not interested in all this self-realisation stuff, it doesn't matter that they have a temper. There are so many people who are not even aware that they are angry people. The very fact that you become aware that you get angry shows that you are a serious person.

Now the question is, how to begin to tackle it? You say yourself that by meditation you are able to bring about a certain change. But you are afraid that if you meditate you are becoming indifferent to the mundane world. However, it is not necessary to become indifferent to the mundane world when you are meditating.

You can meditate and at the same time do your work properly. That is the whole teaching of the *Bhagavad Gita*. For instance, the *karma yoga* teaching is not to become indifferent to the mundane world but to do your work properly, meanwhile continuing your inner development through meditation or *sadhana*. At a point, you become mature enough to decide whether you really want to be indifferent to the world or you don't. By *sadhana*, you would have reached a state when you really understand that the inner is more valuable than the external. Then there will be no conflict whether you are indifferent or not to the mundane world. The conflict indicates that you have still not become sure of the inner. Therefore, till then, give full attention to the world but at the same time, go on increasing your meditation-time and your study-time until you are able to go deeper and deeper into meditation. Then you discover and come across the condition of your mind where you are able to appreciate the inner. In that state you don't become indifferent to the external world because you begin to see the external world as the manifestation of the inner and therefore you are not repulsed by it. On the other hand you begin to work unattached.

Sometimes people think that to do perfect work, you have to be totally attached to it. This is not true. If you can do your work properly without being unduly attached to it, you can perform better than if you are emotionally caught up in it. There was a doctor who had to operate upon his son. He was a well-known doctor and an excellent surgeon. But when it came to operating upon his own son, he decided to call in another surgeon because his sentiments might come in the way of his performance.

If any one of you has gone to learn unarmed combat like *Karate* or *Kung Fu*, you will know that the real expert in unarmed combat does not strike any one in anger because then the blow is bound to miss, or might land harder than expected. The expert is absolutely relaxed. He does not work from his emotions but from his reactions.

Although it is not easy, one must live in the world like a lotus. Although the lotus derives all its nutrition from the water in which it stands, if you sprinkle water on the lotus, it rolls off without a trace. One must live like that. One needs guidance to live like that.

If you begin to meditate and you are aware that temper is a problem, you will certainly be able to solve it, if not in two days, then in two years! One has to work on these things, starting right now.

Q: *Could you kindly explain a little more in detail about the* atman *to be meditated upon by the common man?*
A: Now, this 'common-man' is perhaps not the right term to use. We are all common men! Let us say, '….meditated upon by all.'

To answer the question: one cannot have a common code of meditation for all human beings because each person is made differently, his background is different, his tendencies are different. People may like God with form or without form; some would like a philosophical approach; some might be '*vaishnavites*,' others might be '*shaivites*,' and so on. And so, for each individual, that meditation technique has to be given which is suitable for him. But there is, certainly, a common ground – first, as a take-off point, the agitations of the mind have to be brought under control. Only then one can meditate. With form or without form, *Vishnu, Shiva, Kali* or *Allah* – it does not matter.

The basic thing is to relax the mind, to bring out the agitations of the mind and make them disappear, little by little, until the mind attains a calm state. And for that, one simple technique can be practised by everybody, no matter which path to God he follows. It is what is called 'watching of the breath.' You may want to do *japa* but your mind is not concentrated, it wanders around. That is common.

It is normal for the mind to wander. In the *Gita*, Arjuna asks Krishna: 'You are saying that the mind has to be brought back and kept under control, but I cannot do it. My mind is stronger than the wind. I try to control it but it wanders off. What am I to do?' Krishna tells Arjuna, 'You are not the first person to ask this question. This question has been asked innumerable times. The only way is to bring it back when it wanders, until you become an expert at it.'

One technique of doing this is by what is called *aana pana*, in *vipasana*. It is also taught in *kriya yoga* and in many of the other yogic disciplines. Anybody, also one who has no belief in God, can make his mind calm and quiet. The technique is to sit down quietly, close the eyes and watch one's breath. This is not a casual practice. This particular technique of watching of the breath is taught in great secrecy in some places. Some schools of thought even consider it as the only technique necessary.

'Watching your breath' means to watch it closely. Close your eyes. Do not control the rhythm of the breath. Let it be as it is. Give your attention to it. Just be aware of it. As you inhale, be aware of your inhalation. As you exhale be aware of your exhalation. Continue to watch. Automatically you will find that after sometime the breathing becomes very slow and quiet and when the breathing becomes quiet, the mind also is quietened. You will notice that when you are agitated, your breath has a very disturbed rhythm. When you are calm and quiet – sitting near the sea or listening to music – if you look in and watch your breath, you will see that it has also become calm and quiet. The rhythm has slowed down.

This can be done the other way round to calm your mind. Calm your breath, and the mind also becomes calm. The technique to calm it is to watch it, to observe it. If you observe it, it automatically becomes calm. Normally, we are not aware of our breathing. It takes place involuntarily, automatically. Something is controlling it, not us. It just goes on by itself. Although we pretend to be in total control of our lives, we don't even control our own breath! It is there; when it stops, we come to an end.

Now, if we begin to become aware of that which goes on by itself, then psychologically and spiritually, we move closer to the 'entity' who is controlling the breath. When the breath slows down the mind also slows down. The energy which is normally frittered away in too many activities of the mind is gathered in one place. And after you gather it together, fix it on your *japa*, fix it on your meditation or on whatever you are doing at that moment. You will see how you can really concentrate. That is why, those who have been given the *gayatri mantra* know that before you do the *gayatri, pranayam* is done, because when the breath is brought into a particular rhythm, the mind also automatically follows that rhythm. And when the mind has come to that rhythm, it is possible to fix your attention on what you want. This is the secret.

So, before you meditate upon – form or formless, light, symbol or sound – it will be very helpful if you sit down for a few minutes and watch your breath. In fact, there is a higher, advanced technique of meditation in which the mantra that you chant is coupled with the breath. The *nath panthies* have the famous 'soham' mantra. When they inhale, they chant, 'so' and 'ham' when they exhale. They continue doing this until they reach a state of perfect, crystal clear calmness of the mind.

Q: *How is one to meditate, and when?*
A: How and when to meditate? It is very important to fix a time when you are practising meditation. You cannot say, 'I'll meditate today in the morning and tomorrow at night! Fix a schedule. Don't deviate from that schedule, no matter what happens. Fix a time as early as possible, but not too early, because one day you may get up at 3:30 a.m., the next day you may not be able to do so. If you can get up at 3:30 a.m. every day, it is ideal. Fix a reasonable time early in the morning, so that you are not disturbed, when the air is clear and cool, when it is silent, and the sounds of the day have not begun yet. Open the windows so that air comes in.

Sit easy. It does not matter which side you face, but sit in a quiet place where you are not disturbed. First, look at the world around you. Look at the trees or whatever, and then send a message of love and good-will to all living beings. At least for that period of meditation you have no enemies!

Sit quietly and mentally send a message of love and good wishes to all, and then do your *japa*, or meditation, or watch the breath, whatever it is you have been taught. Fix a time and do that exactly at the same time, if possible at the same place. What happens is that if you sit at a particular time at a particular place and meditate, that place at that time, begets a certain vibration which is built up over the years as you continue. When you go and sit down there, automatically you are in a conducive atmosphere. So it becomes easier to meditate. That is one reason.

The other reason is, if any of you has a link with a teacher or a *guru* who has initiated you, who has given you some *japa* or *mantra*, then it is all the more important that he knows the time when you are sitting, so that he can help you because you are linked. Otherwise, your mind is wandering here and there, and even if he wants to help you, he cannot.

Early morning is the best time. *Brahma muhurat* starts at 3:30, an ideal time but well-nigh impossible for most people! One can at least start at 5 or 5:30 and meditate. Fixing of time and place is very important.

Om Shantih! Om Shantih! Om Shantih!

Kenopanishad

he *Upanishads* are called the *Jnana Kanda* or the 'Wisdom Section' of the *Vedas* and appear after the *Samhitas*. They are also called '*Vedanta*,' which means, 'the end of the *Vedas*' – 'Veda-antah.' A more esoteric interpretation is that it is the understanding that lies 'beyond the words of the *Vedas*,' the Truth behind the words. So, there is a differentiation made between the word and the meaning of the word. This is apt because very often, a word is repeated so many times that it loses its meaning and becomes merely a mechanical repetition.

If the *Upanishads* can be defined at all, one important and simple definition would be by splitting the word '*Upanishad*' into three syllables: *upa* – *ni* – *shad*. *Upa* means, 'to move closer,' 'to go nearer'; *shad* means, 'to sit' and *ni* is the connecting link between 'moving closer' and 'sitting down.' *Ni* represents the level where the disciple sits, a level lower than the teacher. It does not mean sitting physically at a lower level. It means that the student recognizes his level of understanding and comes to the teacher with an open mind; not with the feeling that he has already understood everything. So, he sits in front of the teacher with respect, and listens, in order that he moves closer to the 'Truth.'

Shad means 'sitting down,' not only physically in which the physical act, the *asana*, is involved. It also means the 'settling down of the mind.' If one is sitting down, it means one is settled and is ready to listen. If one were to stand up, it means one is unsettled, and about to walk away. Standing up indicates movement, sitting down indicates rest. *Shad* is 'to settle down quietly', not only physically but also mentally, because the truths of the *Upanishads*, which one is preparing to understand, are so subtle that it is not possible to do so unless and until one has a settled mind. This, roughly, is the meaning of the word, '*Upanishad*.'

The *Upanishads* form the *Jnana Kanda*, which is the wisdom section of the *Vedas*. What do the *Upanishads* deal with exactly? The

Upanishads do not deal with what the *Agamas*, the *Shastras* and the *Brahmanas* deal with, which are the different rituals and daily activities one is supposed to perform in this world. The *Upanishads* deal with what is beyond this. They do not deal with what we normally do but take up universal questions like, 'What is the meaning of life? Where are we going?' and so on. So, if you hope to find tips on how to make money or gain fame in the *Upanishads*, you are looking in the wrong place! There are many other books which can teach this. Even ancient texts like the *Tantras* that say, 'Do this ritual for this benefit and that *pooja* for that benefit' and so on are other sources of advice on these wordly pursuits.

The *Upanishads* are mainly concerned with the universal search of trying to find out the meaning of life – 'What are we moving towards? From birth to death, we keep moving, becoming, evolving. Is there an end to this movement? Is there a meaning to life? Is a human being merely born to live, reproduce and die? Is there some deeper meaning behind all this?' These are the essential questions addressed in the *Upanishads*.

All the *Upanishads* are based on the method of dialogue. They have perhaps the oldest mention of dialogue in world literature. It is a *samvaad* where the disciple goes to the teacher and asks him questions. The teacher does not give him readymade answers. He says, 'Now, this is the guide to find your answer; go and meditate on it.' So the disciple goes, meditates on it, and comes back and says, 'This is what I have found, but I don't think it is the Truth'. Thus it continues, till he arrives at the 'ultimate Truth' with the teacher's help.

If you read any of the *Upanishads*, you will find this method of a continued dialogue, because dialogue is a very important part of understanding. The *Bhagavad Gita* which declares at the end of every chapter, that it is a 'Krishna – Arjuna *samvaada*' is also a dialogue.

Universal questions such as 'What are we seeking?' 'What is our real identity?' are asked and meditated upon by the student. We are born, grow into children, become adolescents and adults, and have children of our own. So at different stages, we are different people. 'Is there something permanent behind all this?' To guide us to the answer, the *Upanishads* examine the three states that we all experience – the waking, dream and deep-sleep states. These states are universal. The *Upanishads* explain that which is permanent, which continues through all these three states.

We have dreams, and when we wake up, we find that the dreams we had were not rooted in reality. We find ourselves in a different state altogether – the waking state. The great sage Janaka Maharaj once had a dream in which he was a beggar, with torn clothes, walking around with a bowl, without food to eat. In the morning, he woke up and found himself in the palace, a king! So he asked his Guru Yajnavalkya that famous question, 'Sir, tell me the truth – am I a beggar or am I a king? Please explain this to me. If the dream had stretched for a longer time, I would have continued to be a beggar and suffered all the difficulties, agony and sorrow. Now that I am awake, I feel that I am the king. Which is the real me?'

Vedanta explains your true identity; that which continues through all three states but which is unaffected by any of them. 'What is my true identity? What am I searching for? Is there an end to this becoming?' These are all basic questions that everyone should ask, at least in this age when we claim we are evolved human beings. This is the subject matter that the *Upanishads* deal with. People dismiss the *Upanishads* as something that is highly complex and difficult to understand. In fact, it is an excuse put forth by the mind which is either too lazy to think, or is afraid of going into deeper aspects because it might lose hold of all the enjoyments it has in the material world. The *Upanishads* are neither too high nor too deep to be comprehended.

The *Kenopanishad*, has a wonderful name. *Kena* means 'By who?' It does not sing the praises of any God or any 'being.' It does not tell us how to find fulfilment in the material world. There are different parts of the *Vedas* that deal with such matters. Here, a question is asked – 'By who?' or, 'Who is behind all this activity that goes on within the personality 'I?' To find one's true identity is the aim of the *Upanishad*.

This *Upanishad* belongs to the *Sama Veda*. The *Sama Veda* is the third of the four *Vedas*. It is a very important *Veda* for various reasons, one of them being that in the *Bhagavad Gita*, when Krishna describes His glories, He says, 'Of the four *Vedas*, I am the *Sama Veda*.' This particular *Upanishad* forms a part of the *Talavakara Brahmana* of the *Sama Veda*. It consists of four short sections – the first two in verse form and the other two in prose.

It is not intended here to deal with the *Kenopanishad, shloka* by *shloka*. Rather, a few selected *shlokas*, chosen from successive sections of the *Upanishad*, will be discussed. The rest shall be taken up together and finally the *Upanishad* summarised.

Before any *Upanishad* starts, there is always an invocation for peace, the *shanti mantra*. The invocation here is:

SHANTI MANTRA

*aum aapayaayantu mamaangaani vaak praanaschakshuh
shrotramatho balamindriyaani cha sarvaani.
sarvam brahmaupanidshadam ma ham brahma niraakuryaam
maa maa brahma niraakarot aniraakaranamastvanira-
karanam mey astu.
tadatmani niratey ya upanishatsu dharmaah tey mayi
santu tey mayi santu.
aum shantih shantih shantih.*

Aapayaayantu mamaangaani vaak pranaschakshu shrotramatho Balamindriyaani cha sarvaani – means, 'May my limbs grow vigorous; may my speech, my breath, my eye, my ear, as also the vitality in all my senses grow vigorous'; 'may my energy be equal in all my senses.'

This shows that the *Upanishads* are not just talking about 'another' world, but of this world also. Unless one is healthy and vigorous, one cannot study the *Upanishads*. They are not something to be studied by people who have dissipated their energies. The invocation itself says, 'May my limbs grow strong; may my mind become strong; may my senses become strong.' The *Mundaka Upanishad* declares, *nayam atma balahineyena labhya;* 'This *atma* cannot be achieved, attained or known by the weak.' It is a message to be strong, to go from strength to strength.

The next part of the invocation is: *Sarvam brahmaupanishadam ma aham brahma niraakuryaam maa maa brahma niraakarot aniraakaranam astva nirakaranam mey astu* – 'all this is the *Brahman* of the *Upanishads*.' The *rishi* who sings this invocation is already aware that everything that he sees is *Brahman*. 'There is nothing other than *Brahman*' – *Sarvang jitat brahma.*

Then the student prays, 'May I never discard *Brahman*, may I never discard the Truth, may I never give up the Absolute Truth nor may *Brahman* discard me.' It is a repetition of a prayer, which shows a complete commitment to the finding of the Truth that is referred to in the *Upanishad* as *Brahman.*

Then it says, *Tadatmani niratey ya upanishatsu dharmaah tey mayi santu. Om Shantih Shantih Shantih,* which means – 'Let the Truth which is set forth in the *Upanishad* live in me; may I grow dedicated to the Self. After every chant, there is *Om Shantih Shantih Shantih!* 'May there be peace, peace, peace!' *Shanti* is something that each one of us is yearning for. Everything else is there, but there is no *Shanti,* no peace of mind! *Shanti* is always at a premium. *Shanti* is what we seek.

So, *'Shantih'* is chanted in the beginning and at the end of the Vedas. Now, here is the first question asked in this *Upanishad*. One might interpret it as the disciple asking the teacher, or the other way round; it could be either. It says:

SECTION ONE: SHLOKA 1

keneshitam patati preshitam manah kena pranah
prathamah praiti yuktah
keneshitaam vaachamimaam vadanti chakshu shrotram
ka u devo yunakti.

Keneshitam patati preshitam manah – 'By whom is the mind activated? When I say, 'I think,' who is it that says 'I think'? Who sits behind the mind and gives the initial thought of, 'I think'? Where does thought originate from?'

The great Ramana Maharshi, who lived in Tiruvannamalai said that a simple way to find out where the thought begins from, the source of thought, is to enquire into the question, 'Where does this 'I' feeling come from?' In fact, he reduced the whole of *Vedanta* into a simple sentence – *deham naaham koham soham. Deham naaham* – 'I am not the body.' If I am not the body, then *koham?* – 'Who am I?' *Soham!* – 'I am 'That'!' That Supreme Brahman which cannot be touched by life or death – 'That' am I!

The question asked is, 'What or who is it that gives the feeling of 'I'? Where is the source of this 'I'? Where does it start?'

Kena pranah prathama praiti yuktah – 'What is it that initiates the first emergence of life, the first movement of life, *pranah*? Where does *pranah* originate from?'

In the *Koran*, when Mohammed got the first revelation, they say the angel who appeared before him said, 'Read!' Mohammed being an illiterate person in the ordinary sense of the term, said, 'I cannot read.' The angel said, 'Read, in the name of God who created man from a clot of blood that issues forth from between the loins!'

So, the question asked in the *Upanishad* is, 'Who is it that originates life, the beginning of life, the first? Who is behind this creation?'

Keneshitaam vaachamimaam vadanti – 'What is it that makes me utter speech? What is the beginning of sound?'

Chakshu shrotram ka u devo yunakti – 'What is this Being that prompts me to see and who prompts me to hear?' Or, 'What is it that sees and hears?'

There is a beautiful *kirtan* in Malayalam, written by a famous writer who was perhaps the earliest of the Malayalam poets. It is called *Hari Naama Sankirtanam*. When we normally say *Hari Naama* and *sankirtanam*, we mean *bhakti or the* singing of *kirtans*, but this *kirtan* is very *Vedantic*. It says,

kanninu kannu, manam aakum kannu atinu kannayidunna porul
tannenarieyumalavu anandam endu hari narayanaya namah.

Kannu means 'eye.' This roughly means, That which is the 'eye' of the eye, that which sees behind the eye, what is that? That is the mind. The mind is the 'eye' of the eye. There is 'something' behind the mind, which sees the mind also, which witnesses the mind. How blissful it is when I understand that 'That' which is also the 'eye' of the mind is my true self! Harinarayanaya Namah!

That was the first question asked. There is actually no answer because there are no readymade answers provided in the *Upanishads*. One has to look into the question deeply and study the *Upanishads* carefully to get some clues. So after this question is asked, the next *shloka* says:

SHLOKA 2

shrotrasya shrotram manaso mano
yad vaacho ha vaacham sa u praanasya praanah
chakshushas chakshur atimuchya dheeraah
prety asmaal lokaat amritaa bhavanti.

That which you are looking for, which is watching the mind, is *shrotrasya shrotram* – 'the 'ear' of the ear.' It is that which hears, when you say that 'the ear hears.' *Manaso mano* – 'It is the 'mind' behind the mind.' It is that which provides the content of the mind.

Yad vaacho ha vaacham – It is the basis from which sound comes forth or language comes forth.' *Sa u praanasya praanah* – 'It is the breath of the breath'; it is that from which *praana* originates. *Chakshushas chakshur* –'It is the 'eye' of the eye.' *Atimuchya dheer-*

aah prety asmaal lokaat amritaa bhavanti – 'The great sages, the wise people, give up their all and reach the higher worlds of immortality.'

Swami Chinmayananda once said that he was sitting in front of Tapovan Maharaj in Uttarkashi and was trying to understand the meaning of the *Upanishad*. When Tapovan Maharaj said, 'It is the 'eye' of the eye, the 'ear' of the ear,' Swami Chinmayananda said, 'Sir, please do not confuse me. Do not say 'this of this and that of that'. Tell me exactly what it is!' Tapovan Maharaj kept quiet for sometime and said, 'We will discuss this later.' Afterwards he said, 'Go and get some water for me from the Ganga.' Swamiji went with his *kamandalu*, collected some water and returned. Tapovan Maharaj flew into a rage and said, 'Who asked you to bring the *kamandalu*? Go get only the water!' Swamiji said, 'Sir, how can I bring the water without the *kamandalu*?' Tapovan Maharaj then made his point: 'Therefore, some *upaadhi*, some instrument, is necessary to bring home the object of the exercise, is it not?'

When we say, 'eye' of the eye and 'ear' of the ear, we are talking about a 'Being' which cannot be grasped by the mind, which cannot even be touched by the intellect. These are abstract truths which require the use of some *upaadhi* to explain the idea; an instrument such as a simile might be used, although even if it is close in meaning, will never be completely accurate because we are not describing a material object.

The *rishi* says, 'Upon understanding that 'Being' who is the 'eye' of the eye and the 'ear' of the ear and the 'mind' of the mind, the wise men 'give up' and attain immortality.' This is a very important statement. What do the wise men 'give up'? When do they 'give up'? One gives up only when one understands the 'valueless-ness' of a thing.

Here, the *rishi* is talking about 'something' which cannot be grasped or touched by the senses. Even to begin understanding this, one must gradually loosen the grip of the senses, because the senses always keep us tied down, covered and bound. The wise who understand this truth, gradually shake off the bondage of the senses. They give up what appears to others to be valuable, but to them is valueless, as they have found what is *really* valuable. We are normally content with the mere tinsel that we see in this world; we hold on to it, not giving up.

Once one understands the emptiness and hollowness of this tinsel, one slowly begins to let go. Only when one lets go, the *rishi* declares, can one comprehend what these words mean: *shrotrasya shrotram* – 'the hearer behind the ear.' Then one reaches immortality, a state where there is no death. This not only means that one goes to a state where one is not reborn, which is what is referred to, but also means that one begins to have the understanding by which one can face death. If one can give up all, then one is ready to face death. The fear that man feels for death is not only because it is something unknown but also because he fears to lose all that he holds near and dear, all that he thinks he deserves to continue to enjoy. If someone were to say that in death we could take with us everything that we enjoyed in this world, then nobody would be afraid of death. Our fear is that we will leave behind everything that we consider to be the most essential for our happiness. When one 'lets go' in life, then there is no fear of 'letting go' in death. So, one faces death squarely.

After saying this, the next question would be, 'Can we reach 'That'? Can we understand this 'Being' who is behind the mind, behind the eye and the ear? Can we understand this 'Being' who is the witness of all that is happening, and by realising whom, one attains immortality? If yes, then how? What is the way?'

By now the student is ready, bristling with expectations, saying, 'How do I get there? Now that I know all this is impermanent, I want to get to the permanent, the immortal. How do I get to it?'

In answer to this, the statement that the *rishi* gives appears even more confusing! The *rishi* declares:

SHLOKA 3 AND 4

na tatra chakshur gacchati na vaag gacchati no manah
na vidmo na vijaaniimo yathaitad anushishyaat
anyad eva tad viditaad atho aviditaad adhi
iti shushruma purveshaam ye nas tad vyaacha chakshirey.

Na tatra chakshur gacchati – 'There the eye does not go'; *na vaag gacchati* – 'nor can words proclaim or understand' what that Supreme Being is. And then, he hits the last nail when he says *no manah* – 'The mind also does not reach there.' There is no other instrument for us – we are left with nothing! When even the mind cannot reach that point, then what is one to do? The agnostic would most likely say, 'Perhaps there is a real Supreme Being, but I am not concerned because one can never reach It!' But that is not the aim of the *Upanishads* – to give you the instrument as if on platter!

The *rishi* declares, *na vidmo na vijaaniimo yathaitad anushishyaat* – 'I am myself confused as to how to teach this to you. It is so difficult to teach that which even the mind cannot reach. How do I express this to you? How do I get this through to you in a manner that you understand?'

So, even in those days, the teacher had to face the difficulty of expressing the subtle truths of the *Upanishads*! When the *rishi* declares '*na tatra chakshur gacchati*', it certainly 'is not something that the physical eye can see'; '*na vaag gacchati*', it certainly 'is not something that words can describe.' Even if one has understood it one does not know how to express it. The reason being that we are talking about a Reality which is of a totally different dimension. We are normally accustomed to thinking in three dimensional forms having length, breadth and height, and cannot conceive of forms having a fourth or a fifth dimension of which we know nothing. Even if conceived, it is difficult to express them in three dimensional language. People who are into advanced Mathematics or Quantum Physics will appreciate what is being said here!

So the *rishi* says, 'The mind also cannot reach there.' After the Master expresses his difficulty in not being able to describe the Truth, because it is 'That' which the mind cannot reach, he brings in the teaching of the *Vedanta*, which is through negation. This is what Shankaracharya declared as the *neti neti* method – 'not this, not this!' Anything that is born and dies cannot be permanent; anything that is created is not permanent. Therefore, none of these things can be the 'Truth,' since we are looking for a changeless permanent reality. The mind thinks of many things and keeps moving and changing all the time. So the *Upanishads* say, 'not this, not this.' Everything has thus been negated in order to arrive at what is real. Now, this is something which one has to practise in real life. The *Upanishads* are not theoretical texts. When one looks at everything in totality and sees the impermanence of life – the sorrow, the pain, the suffering, and ultimately, death, then one begins to negate and say, 'if there is a Supreme Reality, it is not any of these things.' The *Upanishad* declares, 'It cannot be touched by the mind.' So whatever I imagine, however big, however large, however extended, it cannot be the Truth. So, that is also negated. When everything is negated, what happens? Does the mind become blank?

If the Truth cannot be understood at all, one would say, 'Let us drop this exercise, let us leave it at that!' But the *rishi* does not leave you there. He says, *anyad eva tad viditaad atho aviditaad adhi iti shushruma purveshaam ye nas tad vyaacha chakshirey* – 'We have heard from the ancients who have explained to us that It is indeed other than the known; but It is not the unknown either!' So do not think that It is something that can never be known. That is what the *rishi* means. There is hope that we can find the answers! Only, these answers cannot be known by the instruments which are normally adopted for empirical learning, or by the knowledge of what we see in the material world.

On the other hand, *anyad eva tad viditaad; atho aviditaad adhi* – 'it is not the unknown; not something that cannot be known'. It can be known, but not by the instruments normally used to understand the universe of matter and also the universe of thought. So, is there some other instrument? The *rishi* takes up each of the known 'instruments,' one by one, which 'the eye does not see nor can words proclaim.'

SHLOKA 5

yad vaachaa nabhyuditam yena vaag abhyudyate
tad eva brahma tvam viddhi nedam yad idam upaasate.

'That which is not expressed through speech, but by which speech is expressed' – *yad vaachaa nabhyuditam yena vaag abhyudyate*. It is the origin of speech, but speech cannot express it. Then the *rishi* makes an extraordinary statement – *tad eva brahma tvam vidhi nedam yad idam upaasate* – 'Therefore understand, that alone is *Brahman*, nothing that you worship here!' This statement is of great significance. 'Understand, that alone is Brahman, which speech cannot express but is the source of speech' – *tad eva brahma tvam viddhi*: 'Understand you, that alone is *Brahman*.' *Nedam yad idam upaasate*: 'Nothing that you worship here!' This sounds nihilistic! When Adi Shankaracharya started giving his talks and having discussions, the religious orthodoxy, which was mostly involved with the ritualistic portions of the *Vedas* and not the *jnana* section, called him a *pracchanna bouddhika* – 'a Buddhist in disguise!' At that time, Buddhism was prevalent in the country, and the orthodox priests who controlled public religiosity felt uncomfortable with this and said, 'As it is, Buddhism has made many people atheists; now here is someone who is trying to make us all atheists through our own *Upanishads* by saying, 'Nothing that you worship here is *Brahman*'!' Shankaracharya wrote commentaries on all the main *Upanishads*, yet they thought he was trying to destroy Hinduism!

What *Vedanta* says is, not that there is no such reality, but that that reality has nothing to do with anything that you worship outside yourself. When you say *upaasate*, 'worship,' it is not only worshipping an image or a picture. It also means cherishing all the material things of life which we consider to be important, all the mental imagery and the feelings which we have built up and come to adore and worship. None of them is the Truth – 'understand this!'

SHLOKA 6

yan manasaa na manute yenaahur mano matam
tad eva brahma tvam viddhi nedam yad idam upaasate

'That which cannot be thought of by the mind' – *yan manasaa na manute*. The mind cannot think of it but because of it, the mind acquires the capacity to think.

Tad eva Brahma tvam viddhi – 'That alone is the 'Truth,' the *Brahman*.' *Nedam yad idam upaasate* – 'nothing that you worship here, nothing that you adore here'. When we say, 'I adore something' or 'I worship something,' three things are involved – the worshipper, the worshipped and the act of worship. If you are looking for the 'Supreme, Unconditioned Self,' the *Brahman*, then these three separate entities are not required.

Now, please understand that the *Upanishad* is not saying, 'Don't worship,'! Worship is indeed required with a different level of understanding. Even Shankaracharya, after having written commentaries on the *Upanishads*, established temples because they were necessary for another level of understanding. Everyone cannot start swimming in the ocean right away, but have to be led to that stage gradually, in steps. But, when you begin to seriously understand the 'Supreme Truth,' these intermediate steps are not important. This is very significant. So it is said, 'That which the mind cannot understand, grasp or express, but because of which the mind exists, 'That' alone is the 'Truth', please understand, nothing that you adore here!'

Then, the last *shloka* in this Section:

SHLOKA 7

yat praanena na praaniti yena praanah praniyate
tad eva brahma tvam viddhi nedam yad idam upaasate.

'That which is not breathed by life, but, by which life breathes.' It is the origin of all life. 'That alone is the Supreme *Brahman*, know this, nothing that you adore or worship here!'

The third *shloka* of the second section is particularly important here:

SECTION TWO: SHLOKA 3

yasyaamatam tasya matam matam yasya na veda sah
avijnaatam vijaanataam vijnaatam avijaanataam

'Those who think they know, do not know, and those who think they do not know, perhaps do know! It is not understood by those who think they understand it; it is perhaps understood by those who think they do not understand!' Apparently, this is a pardoxical and an illogical statement. But the idea is to make a person think.

If the Supreme Being, which is our essential identity, the real 'I' behind our personality, the mask we wear; if that 'I,' that Supreme Being is infinite, it cannot be touched or understood by the senses or the mind. That is what the *rishi* means by saying, 'It cannot be known.' The one who says, 'I have known It,' or, 'I have understood It,' has used the senses, and therefore couldn't have known It.

There is a very great secret behind this statement. This is how the *Upanishad*, in its own way, comes from something very transcendental to something very real and actual. When I say, 'I know something,' the 'I,' the ego, is getting strengthened. When this centre, the 'I,' is gone, then what remains is the Supreme Truth.

In *bhakti* there is not only singing of *kirtans, bhajans* and other acts of devotion, as most people think it to be. *Bhakti* is essentially an attitude by which a person begins to understand the limitations of the movement of the intellect. When the intellect begins to understand how limited its reach is, then it cuts itself out. It becomes absolutely silent. When fancy can no more unfurl its wings, when it settles down, then what remains is the experience of the Supreme Self. That means, the little 'I' has to go. Someone once told me that the shortest cut is to cut the ego into two! That is easier said than done!

It was explained how anything that you know, in the ordinary sense, is merely knowledge that is stored in the memory, and therefore, not a thing which is in the present. You recall it, and then you say, 'I have the knowledge of it.' But the Supreme Being, if one has to know at all, is always present now, at this moment! It is nothing that can be stored in the memory. Therefore, it cannot be known in the usual mode, like when we say, 'I know something, I have understood something.' This understanding is a permanent affair. Once understood, always understood!

Now we come to an important part, the last *shloka* in the second section:

SHLOKA 5

iha ched avedid atha satyam asti na ched ihaavedin
mahati vinashtih
bhuteshu bhuteshu vichintya dhiiraah pretyaasmal
lokaad amritaa bhavanti

'If a person knows it here, then there is 'Truth'. If he does not know it, there is great loss.'

This *shloka* shows that the main purpose of the great souls has been to understand the higher mysteries of life. It is also a warning not to postpone the knowledge of 'Brahman.' Most people feel that there are many other things to do, more important than the search for Truth. But we must realise that life can end at any moment, and therefore there is an urgency to know the reason why we live, what we live for and who we are. The sooner we realise this the better, because one never knows what the future holds for us. If I came to know somehow that I was going to die the next day, or in a week's time, what would I do? Would I go around trying to collect things which I cannot take with me, or would I sit down and think, 'Where am I going? What is in store after this life? Who am I?'

So, urgency is required. It has to be *now*. Ramakrishna Paramahamsa had these lovely little aphorisms by which he would illustrate great truths. 'You cannot swim in the ocean straightaway; first, you have to start in a little pool.' Practise in the small pool. Start the practice now, with a sense of urgency.

'If it is known, there is 'Truth'; if it is not known, there is great loss.'

Now to the third section:

SECTION THREE: SHLOKA 1

brahma ha devebhyo vijigye tasya ha brahmano vijaye deva
amahiiyanta ta aikshanta asmaakam evaayam vijayo
asmaakam evaayam mahimaa iti.

After all this abstraction, there comes a little story, an allegory. This is something great about the *Upanishads* and the sacred books of all religions. After talking what appears to be total abstraction, the *rishi* takes up a little story, for it is easier to relate to a story and thereby understand the Supreme Being.

The story begins – 'Once *Brahman* conquered for the gods.' The gods are the different powers of nature. They get their power to perform from *Brahman*. When we say that 'the gods have conquered something,' it means that they have been given the strength to conquer by the *Supreme Brahman*. (Even in this world, forgetting this universal truth, when someone does something significant one feels, 'Ah! I have done this!')

Similarly, when these gods had achieved victory, they thought that it was they who had achieved it and forgot that they got the powers to do so from *Brahman*. Without *Brahman*, there is no power, no energy. The whole vitality comes from 'That.' But the gods congratulated themselves. 'We have achieved all this. This victory is ours, this greatness is ours!' (Would they have blamed themselves, had they lost?)

To illustrate this point furthur:

Sri Ramakrishna was very fond of the story about the brahmin and the cow. There was a brahmin who had a beautiful garden. He looked after it very well and with great pride. He would take visitors and talk about the flowers and plants. One day, a cow came in through the fence and ate up some of the flowers. In a fit of anger the brahmin killed the cow! He did not want people to know this, so he dug a pit and buried it under a small mound. The brahmin had committed the sin of *gohatya* and tried to hide it. One day, Indra came in disguise, and the brahmin proudly showed him around the garden. When he asked him about the mound, the brahmin said, 'Oh! That was done by Indra!', because anger is associated with Indra, not with a brahmin! When we do bad actions we like to hide them. When we do good actions we like to take the credit.

Seeing the attitude of the gods, the all-pervading Supreme Being, *Brahman*, decided to teach them the Truth.

SHLOKA 2

tadd haishaam vijajnau tebhyo ha praadur babhuva
tan na vyajaanata kim idam yaksham iti

Brahman appeared before the gods in the form of a *Yaksha*, an adorable spirit. He wanted to test their conceit. He knew that they were proud of themselves and had forgotten from where their power originated. This is the importance of this allegory. As long as we are proud of ourselves and do not remember where all the energy comes from, we are stuck; we do not know *Brahman* although we may think we do.

When *Brahman* appeared before the gods they did not know who that Being was. The gods could not perceive the Supreme Being before them, as they were caught up in the proud feeling that the victory was their achievement.

SHLOKA 3

tey agnim abruvan jaataveda etad
vijaanihi kim etad yaksham iti tatheti

Agni – Fire, is called *jaatavedas* – 'the knower of the *Vedas*.' The gods knew that Agni had studied the *Vedas*, 'swallowed' them and knew their meaning. So he was chosen to go and and find out who this *Yaksha*, this Being, was. Agni agreed. He was to soon find out that the knowledge of the *Vedas* is not enough to know the Supreme Being, *Brahman*.

The Mundaka *Upanishad* speaks of *paraa vidya and aparaa vidya*. It says every branch of knowledge, including the *Vedas* and the *Shastras*, is *aparaa vidya*; only by the *paraa vidya* can one know *Brahman*, the Supreme Being.

SHLOKA 4

tad abhyadravat tam abhyavadat ko asi iti agnir
va aham asmi iti abravit jaati veda va aham asmi iti.

Agni went to find out who that Being was. He rushed towards the Yaksha in all his glory, in full blaze. The Being asked, 'Who are you?' *Agni* said, 'I am *Agni*. I am *jaatavedas* – the knower of the *Vedas*!'

SHLOKA 5

tasmin stvayi kim veeryam iti api idam
sarvam daheyam yad idam prithivyaam iti.

The Supreme *Brahman* said, 'So, what power is there in you?'
This was a test. *Agni* replied, 'I can burn down anything, even the
whole *prithvi* – earth!' *Agni* had not yet understood that the power
of burning which he had came from the Supreme Being. He had
not seen the Supreme Being and did not know about It.

SHLOKA 6

tasmai trnam nidadhau etad daheti
tad upapreyaaya sarvajavena tanna shashaaka dagdhum
sa tata eva nivavrte
naitad ashakam vijnaatum yad etad yaksham iti.

The Supreme Being put a blade of grass before *Agni* and said,
'If you can burn down the universe, then burn this!' *Agni* blew fire
with all his might, from every side, but that little blade of grass
would not burn. Try as he might, *Agni* could not burn it. He came
back to his fellow gods and said, 'I do not know who that Yaksha is!
I could not find out!'

SHLOKA 7

atha vayum abruvan vaayav etad vijaanihi
kim etad yaksham iti tatha iti

Then the gods called the next powerful god, *Vayu*. They said,
'O *Vayu*, you go now and find out who this Yaksha is.' *Vayu* agreed
quite confidently although he saw that *Agni* could not burn even a
blade of grass that was placed in front of him.

SHLOKA 8

tad abhyadravat tam abhyavadat ka asi iti
ayur va aham asmi iti
abraveen maatarishvaa aham asmi iti.

And *Vayu* went towards the Yaksha, the Supreme Being, who asked him, 'Who are you?' *Vayu* replied, 'I am Vayu, *Maatarishva*, the one who trods the skies!'

SHLOKA 9

tasmins tvayi kim veeryam iti api idam
sarvam daheyam yad idam prithivyaam iti.

Brahman said, 'And what is the power within you?' *Vayu* replied, 'I can blow away everything, whatever there is on earth!'

SHLOKA 10

tasmai trnam nidaahau etad aadatsveti tad upapreyaaya
tarvajavena tan na shashaaka datum sa tata eva
nivavrte naitad ashakam vijnaatum yad etad yaksham iti.

The *Yaksha* placed a blade of grass before him and said, 'Then blow this away!' *Vayu* tried with all his might to blow off the grass, but it did not move at all. So he came back to the gods and said in amazement, 'I don't know what that Being is!'

SHLOKA 11

athendram abnuvan maghavan etad vijaaniihi kim etad
yaksham iti tatheti tad abhyadravat tasmaat tirodadhe.

The gods approached *Indra*, the king of gods. *Indra* also represents the five senses. He is also called *Maghavan* – he who has wealth and power. They asked him to find out who the great Being was, because *Agni*, the god of fire, and *Vayu*, the god of air, had failed to do so.

In the practical context of *sadhana*, *Agni* or 'fire' means 'the fire of meditation'; it also means 'the digestive fire.' *Vayu* is *prana* or 'breath' and *Indra* represents the 'five senses.' So, since *Agni* and *Vayu*, the powers of nature, tried to find *Brahman* and could not, they said, 'Now let the lord of the senses, *Indra* try it!' Indra agreed. As he reached there, the Yaksha disappeared. That means the senses cannot see the Being. Compared to the other powers of nature, the senses are superior. The senses capture the impressions of whatever we perceive and experience. Although they cannot see the Supreme being, they are able to at least understand the fact that they cannot!

It should be understood from the *shloka* that the senses are not being belittled. They have their own uses. The *Upanishad* only says, 'Sharpen the senses!' and not, 'Cut them out!' When *Indra*, who represents the senses in their usual form, tried to understand the Supreme Being, he could not. The Being simply disappeared.

And then what happened?

SHLOKA 12

sa tasminn eva aakaashe striyam aajagaama bahu shobhamaanaam
umaam haimavatiim tam ha uvaacha kim etad yaksham iti.

The moment the Supreme Being disappeared, something extraordinary happened. A beautiful and charming lady, the 'Daughter of the Himalayas' suddenly appeared before *Indra*. *Indra* asked Her, 'Do you know who this Being is?'

This is very significant. The *rishi* brings us from the abstract to the concrete. Till now, he was talking of abstraction, powers, and senses. Now, we have a form coming down as the 'Daughter of Himalayas.' The Himalayas are the abode of the *rishis*, the great ones, and also of Lord *Shiva* who resides in *Kailash*.

So here appears *Uma*, 'the Daughter of the Himalayas.' She comes to teach *Indra*, lord of the senses. This is symbolic. The *Upanishad* is trying to say that abstractions can be understood through the concrete. When the senses represented by Indra, and the mind represented by Uma, come together and begin to understand the manifestation of the Supreme in concrete form, then a beginning is made, because one cannot understand the Supreme Being directly. One has to start with the faculties that one has. One cannot 'leap' or 'jump' because the mind cannot reach it directly.

Indra asks *Uma*, 'What is It? Who is this Being who was here? We all tried to know Him but could not. We could not even touch the blades of grass He placed before us. Who is this Being?'

Uma's reply is in section four:

SECTION FOUR: SHLOKA 1

saa brahmeti hovaacha brahmano vaa etad vijaye mahiyadvam iti
tato haiva vidaa chakaara brahma iti.

'That was indeed the *Brahman*. It is His victory for which you glorify yourselves. It is because of that Supreme Being's power that you are victorious but, thinking that they are your victories, you, feel joyous and proud.'

'Understand that the Supreme Being, whom you cannot find, is the cause. It is because of Him that you function!'

SHLOKA 2

tasmaad va ete deva atitaraamivaanyaan
devaan yad agnin vayun indrahte hy enan nedishtham
pasprushuh te hy enat prathamo vidaam chakaara brahma iti.

These gods, *Agni, Vayu* and *Indra* are considered to be higher than the rest because they went closest to *Brahman*. *Indra* was the one who first knew about It, even though he could not see It, and therefore he is considered to be supreme among the gods. He was the first one who knew about the existence of the Supreme Being through the revelation by *Uma*.

There is a lovely story from the life of Sri Ramakrishna which has some relevance to this allegory. The person who initiated him into *Vedanta*, Totapuri, was a great *Paramahamsa sanyasin* who, having got rid of everything, did not even wear any clothes. Totapuri was a huge man in contrast to Sri Ramakrishna. When Totapuri came to Dakshineshwar, Ramakrishna had already had the vision of God in the form of Mother Kali – *Shakti*. Totapuri came there and said, 'I have come looking for a person to teach *Vedanta*. From your face, I think you are a fit person.'

Sri Ramakrishna said, 'Wait a minute. Let me first ask my Mother!' Totapuri was a *paramahamsa sanyasin*, a pure *Advaitin*, who only believed in *Brahman* and was not bothered about *Shakti* or anything else – *Brahma satyam jagat mithya*. So he thought that Sri Ramakrishna was going to ask his mother who might be somewhere inside the house. Sri Ramakrishna went to Kali, the Divine Mother, whom he worshipped and got her permission. He came back to Totapuri and said, 'Yes, I will learn from you.'

Totapuri belonged to that order of *sanyasins* who do not stay for more than three days in one place because they do not want to get caught up with anything. But Totapuri lived for over three months with Sri Ramakrishna because he found that Ramakrishna could achieve the state of *nirvikalpa samadhi* in three days, something which took Totapuri forty years to achieve! So he stayed on with him, watching him in wonder.

At the end of his stay, he had such a severe stomach ache that he could not concentrate to get into his meditation or *samadhi*. Being a great *paramahamsa* who did not care for his body, he said to himself, 'If I cannot fix my mind, this body is useless! Let me give it up!' He walked into the Ganges. It is said that however deep into the water he went, he could not reach deep enough to drown himself. So he came back, and Ramakrishna said, 'If only you could accept the 'Mother' as an agent, you might get rid of your problem. You need not accept her as the Supreme Being, but as the link to the Supreme Being.' Finally, Totapuri is believed to have accepted *Shakti*, and left. Perhaps it was ordained that he should go to Dakshineshwar to understand from Sri Ramakrishna that *Shakti* and *Shivam, Prakriti* and *Purusha*, are two sides of the same coin, like fire and its power to burn. They are not two things; one cannot separate them.

Going back to the *Upanishad*, these gods – *Agni, Vayu* and *Indra,* are called the greatest among the gods because they went closest to *Brahman*. *Indra* is the greatest among them because he was the first to learn that That invisible Supreme Being was the Brahman.

SHLOKA 4

tasyaisha aadesho yad etad vidyuto vyadyutadaa
itiin nyamiimishadaa iti adhidaivatam.

The description of *Brahman* that 'it is like a flash of lightning' or 'it is like the blink of an eye' – what does this mean? It is not that the *Brahman* flashes like lightning. It is also not a reference to the lights one sees in meditation. This is only an example which the *rishi* gives, to say that the realization of the Supreme *Brahman* is not something that one achieves in a fixed time. It is also not something that one can attain, which may then be lost forever. I cannot say, 'I will get it in time. I am working towards it and I will understand it after a few days!'

When it actually takes place, when one understands perfectly, the realization of *Brahman* comes 'like a flash.' No time is required, not even the time it takes to blink! It is not something that one achieves in due course of time.

Then what does one achieve in due course? What is the meaning of all the *sadhana* that one does? That is the preparation, the movement towards making the mind steady, quiet, peaceful and still. Once that is done, the actual realization takes place once for all, as fast as a flash of lightning and as spontaneously as it comes across the dark sky. It is not something that can be imitated later, in the sense that the mind comes to know of it once and then easily experiences it again and again. When one does the *sadhana* that one has been taught – the meditation, chanting *japa* and so on, one is preparing the ground for the understanding of the Supreme Being. You are keeping the room in order; sweeping it, cleaning it, clearing the cobwebs, opening the windows, pulling the curtains – you are ready! Then, infinite patience is required. The breeze is definitely going to blow in. When it will come, nobody knows! When it comes, it comes in a flash!

That is why all this preparation is necessary; otherwise, when the breeze of understanding comes, our windows and doors are shut. *Sadhana* opens these out. Now, since it cannot be known through the senses or the mind, there definitely is some other instrument through which one knows it and that has been called 'intuition,' or 'inspiration.' That can come about only when the mind has settled down and stopped all its acrobatics, trying to reach here and there, going inside and outside. Everything has to stop. *Sadhana* is a preparation for that.

If it is going to be always unknown, there would be no point studying the *Upanishads*. But to be in a position to read and understand the subtle truths in the *Upanishads*, the mind must first get still and stop its wandering. *Sadhana* helps us to achieve that by sitting down quietly for a few minutes everyday, closing our eyes and watching our thoughts or doing our *japa*. This is necessary. Some might feel that since 'it comes in a flash,' all this is not necessary. But, we must ask ourselves, are we ready to see the flash when it comes?

So, that is one of the teachings. This *Brahman* is like 'a flash of lightning' or like 'the blink of an eye' for which one must prepare oneself when it comes.

SHLOKA 5

atha adhyatmam yadetat gacchativa cha manah
anena chaitad upasmaraty abheekshnam sankalpah.

This shloka discusses the nature of the Essential Self, the *Atman*. It is towards this that the mind appears to move. We all desire happiness. Every sane human being looks for happiness, not pain. Even if one goes through a lot of pain, one does so in the hope that, at the end of it, there is happiness. The *rishi* says that this movement of the mind towards happiness is actually a movement towards the Supreme Self, which, in us, is the *atman*. But not knowing the right direction, it goes in the wrong direction. It can be steered in the right direction when one understands the impermanence of the world, when one sees the hollowness of existence. Then one begins to think 'Maybe it is elsewhere that we should seek happiness.' Then, one stops and turns around. It is a difficult process. It is difficult because you become one of the few who turn around and go upstream while everyone else moves downstream.

It is because of the power of the Self that the mind is able to remember. What we call will power, or volition, is also the power of the Supreme Being, although we would like to think that it is the power of our minds.

The *rishi* says that when the mind moves towards happiness in the world, it is actually moving in the wrong direction. Kabirdas has this wonderful story about the musk deer. In the breeding season, the deer produces musk – *kasturi* – in a little bag under its tail. When the fragrance begins to waft around it, the poor deer goes looking for the source everywhere, imagining that it comes from somewhere outside but not knowing that it emanates from itself.

Similarly, we look for happiness all around us; everywhere but within us!

We are now at the end of the *Upanishad*, and a synopsis of what has been covered is useful. The *Kenopanishad* is a very important *Upanishad*. The word 'kena' means, 'By who?' It proceeds to ask the question, 'Who is behind all that we see, all that we hear, all that we experience? Who is the experiencer or witness of all that is happening?' This witness remains unaffected by all these things that happen. 'Unaffected,' in the sense that it is 'not touched by' or 'not corrupted by' anything.

By asking the question, *keneshitam patati preshitam manah* (By whom is the mind activated?), the Upanishads proceeds to guide the questioner towards the answer and lead him step by step. Though the steps appear confusing at first, finally the matter seems to clear up!

As mentioned earlier, there is in the *Upanishads* a way of teaching, which is very close to *Zen*, where the questions are not posed to get readymade answers. The questions are made to sink into the very consciousness of the person, so that the answers come out by themselves, because, according to *Vedanta*, the Truth cannot be experienced by anyone other than the person himself. It cannot be given on a platter. A readymade Truth cannot be fed to anybody. It has to come by one's own realization. Therefore, the answers have to be found by you. You cannot even depend upon what has been written in books, even a book like the *Upanishads*. The *Mundaka Upanishad* declares that all the four *Vedas*, for instance, belong to what is called *aparaa vidya*, which cannot take you to the Reality.

The *rishis* declare that it is not through any verbal knowledge or understanding, but only through deep, intuitional understanding, that transcends the working of the brain, that one can realize the Self.

Na tatra chakshur gacchati na vaag gacchati no manah: "There the eye cannot go, neither words can describe it, nor can the mind touch it.' So, we are looking for something that the usual instruments, the usual modes of obtaining knowledge cannot reveal. Therefore, says the *Upanishad*, when the 'limited mind' which seeks settles down, when the mind becomes free and the ego is surrendered and finished with, then what remains is the Supreme Being.

The mind seeks because it sees sorrow, it sees pain, it sees trouble. It thinks, it gets fed up and says, 'Let me get out of this entrapment!' The seeker, the limited self, is a part of this cycle of pain and pleasure, and the limited personality is trying to get out of its own pain and sorrow. When that seeker himself 'ceases to exist' – we are not talking about 'physical death' but the 'finishing of the ego' – then the seeker discovers that the seeking of the Supreme Being cannot be done by reaching out, but by settling down.

That is also one of the definitions of the word *Upanishad*. Shankaracharya has translated the word *shad* as 'shaking-up,' 'loosening the hold.' What 'holds' the mind is mainly desire, desire by the senses to possess sensual objects desired by the imagination, and other attractions. When the anchor of the mind's desire is 'shaken up' and 'loosened' the mind becomes free. What remains is the Supreme Being. It is not as if one can become the Supreme Being. The Supreme Being already 'Is' – one has to remove the veils. It is almost like the sculptor who takes a slab of stone and starts chipping away at it. He chips off what is not necessary and what is left is the image that he wants. He does not add anything from outside. In the Vedantic process of learning, more than adding, chipping away is important. Removing the veil, rubbing out what is not necessary and getting to what remains. This is why this method is called the *neti neti* method – 'it is not this, it is not this.' Then at one point, you come to the absolute end of negation. What remains is what we are seeking.

This is the message well illustrated by the allegory in which *Brahman*, the Supreme Being, once appeared before the gods as the unknown *Yaksha*. *Agni*, *Vayu* and *Indra* – all the powerful forces of nature go to find out who He is. They had been rejoicing in their victory over evil forces and had become very proud and reveled in the glory of it. They did not know that their victory was actually the victory of the Supreme Being, without whom they had no power whatsoever.

From high philosophy and abstract metaphysics, the discussion comes down to actuality, the ego. But it comes down so gradually and so imperceptibly that one has to catch it. That is why the knowledge of the *Upanishads* is supposed to be very subtle. That is why, when the brahmin chants his *gayatri* early in the morning, his only request is – *dhiyo yo nah prachodayaat* – 'stimulate my intellect; make by intellect subtle; may I understand the supreme wisdom of the *Upanishads*.' Even for studies in higher mathematics, science, and other subjects, one has to have a subtle mind. To attain this, the essence of all knowledge, one obviously has to approach it with great humility and attention. This humility and attention is also a kind of affection, the love of knowledge. The love for knowledge and the desire to understand must be there. When that kind of all consuming love comes, then one is not worried about anything else. Whole-hearted attention is given because the seriousness of the problem is realized.

Now, coming back to the allegory: the gods try to find out, unsuccessfully, what the Supreme Being is. The Supreme Being puts a blade of grass in front of them. He asks *Agni* to burn it and he fails; He asks *Vayu* to blow it off and he fails. Then comes *Indra*, the lord of the senses, but as he approaches, the *Yaksha* disappears.

This suggests two things. One, the senses are those which can go closest to the 'Truth,' because it is through the experience of the senses that one even begins to think and understand that something exists beyond the senses. If we did not see, or hear, we would not know what it is to not see or hear. So, the senses are not things to be neglected or belittled. They are to be properly used, not abused and dissipated. This is the importance of *sadhana*; the senses are properly used and sharpened and not neglected, as the very *Shanti mantra* of the *Kenopanishad* says, 'May our limbs grow vigorous, may our senses grow vigorous, may our mind have the energy to look within.' The senses are there for use, not abuse.

The other point is that the senses can go closest, but they cannot see or feel or experience the Supreme Being and so they return. Then the Supreme Being, in the form of the *Yaksha*, disappears. Then comes the most beautiful manifestation of wisdom in the form of *Uma* – *Haimavatim bahu shobhamaanaam* – of indescribable beauty, this 'daughter of the Himalayas!' She says to the gods, 'The *Yaksha* was *Brahman* Himself, whose victory you thought was yours. Understand this!' She becomes the medium to guide the seeker to the Supreme Being.

There is great meaning in presenting the teacher in feminine form. Feminine characteristics are unique; men cannot even understand them adequately. A woman is one who receives and gives in plenty. This aspect of *Shakti* has always been very important. Perhaps the earliest reference to *Shakti* or *Uma* comes in this *Upanishad*. She is beautiful, which means beauty is not a thing to be shunned. As one progresses, when one finds the inner beauty, the inner truth, then one begins to feel that everything is beautiful! Then there is no 'inner' and 'outer'. There is only One!

In the beginning of *sadhana*, the attraction to the form is often necessary in order to be guided into the formless. This is a question of practical *sadhana* because one cannot jump to or fix one's mind on the abstract reality, something in thin air, although ultimately it is the formless that we seek. On the other hand, if one learns to gather one's energies into one center or one form, or one ideal, then at some point, one may reach a stage when one may drop the form. So a form, especially an attractive form, is necessary for one to be able to fix one's mind on one point, and then, when one comes to a certain state, one may choose to discard it. It is like making an image out of clay. Clay has no shape as such. You put the clay into a mould and press it until the image sets, and then you break the mould for the image to emerge.

In Section Four, the *Upanishad* describes, through the words of *Uma*, the experience of *Brahman*. It is not a gradual formation, not a gradual experience, but a sudden flash, like that of lightning or like the blink of an eye. It is not an experience that is collected in the memory and retained. It is a present experience which, as the *Upanishad* says, 'If you understand it now, there is bliss; if you do not understand it at this moment, it is a disastrous loss.' So the *Upanishad* is speaking of the present, not of some future date when one can attain it, as some think.

The fourth *shloka* of Section Four is: *Tasyaisha aadesho yad etad vidyuto vyadyutadaa itiin nyamiimishadaa ity adhidaivatam.*

This speaks about *Brahman.* It means that, 'It is like a flash of lightning.' When illumination comes, it comes like a flash of lightning. No one can say when it will come. One has to be prepared for it because it can come anytime. This is the teaching concerning the Gods because it happened to the Gods *Agni, Vayu* and *Indra. Brahman* appeared before them and disappeared suddenly before they could catch It.

The issue is, 'Can you catch it when it comes, or will you miss it?' Every postponement of trying to find the Supreme Being is a failure, a loss, because it flashes, and it is gone! One has to be alert enough to catch it.

From birth to death, thought is a continuous process. The mind chatters and moves endlessly. It appears that there is hardly any gap between one thought and another. Of course, we cannot find that gap normally, but if you could grasp that junction, then you have it, in the blink of an eye. Like the *Upanishad* says, *iti shushruma purveshaam:* 'Thus we have heard from the ancients.'

The fifth *shloka: Athaadhyaatmam yadetat gacchativa cha manah anena chaitad upasmaraty abhikshanam sankalpah.*

This is the teaching about the 'Self,' the *atma.* The mind always goes towards and moves towards the 'Self,' being attracted by it. It is also that which the mind remembers constantly. *Sankalpah* is 'volition' – the will to do something; the decision to do something, 'I want to do something'. This is part of the working of the 'Self.'

We all desire happiness. The mind in all of us moves towards material happiness, and that movement, say the *Upanishads*, is actually a movement towards the 'Self,' but in the opposite direction. If we understand this and change the direction of this movement, then, happiness can actually be found. When we look inwards, we come back to the source of eternal happiness.

When a person enjoys something, the enjoyment is in that person, not in the thing being enjoyed. For instance, when one smells perfume, it is lovely; when one hears a beautiful song, it is wonderful; when one eats good food, it is tasty – one enjoys it all. When the song reaches the ear, its vibrations come into contact with the eardrum. When the food reaches the mouth, it comes into contact with the taste buds, the sensory organs of taste. Now, where is the enjoyment taking place? It is within the person, not in the song or the food, not even in the organs of hearing or taste. Indeed, this is why the same song or the same food does not appeal to all who hear or taste it. Indeed, the same song if heard over and over, or the same food if eaten again and again, loses its appeal! In the same way, for all sensory enjoyments, the enjoyment is actually in me, although the enjoyment is triggered off when that particular sense organ is in touch with that particular sensation.

The *rishi* says that the reservoir of all this enjoyment, of happiness, is within you. It is being manifested in small portions when the sensory organs come into contact with those particular senses. Therefore, when man yearns for bliss, for happiness, he is actually moving towards the 'Self,' although he thinks he is moving outward. If you can retrace and go within, you can enjoy the whole reservoir of bliss. The basis, the essence, the source of all bliss, can be found if the mind turns back. And then one no longer bothers about the little manifestations of bliss as enjoyed by the senses.

The sixth *shloka* is a more detailed explanation of what was said before.

SHLOKA 6

*tadd ha tadvanam naama tadvanam iti upaasitavyam sa ya etad
evam vedaabhi hainang sarvaani bhutaani samvaanchanti.*

The verse says:
Brahman, the object of all desire, is the most precious of all.
External objects look like something today and something else to-
morrow. They will die and disappear, but the human life constantly
continues with this desire – call it affection, love, attraction or lust.
In fact, when someone says, 'I love you,' actually it is not 'you' but
the 'Self' within! The great sage Yagnavalkya reveals this to his wife
Maitreyi in the *Brihadaranyaka Upanishad.*

Tadd ha tadvanam naama – 'that which is given the name of
tadvanam – the most precious of all.' That is the 'Supreme Self,' the
object of all desire, which man mistakenly seeks outside himself.

This is to be meditated upon – *tadvanam iti upaasitavyam*:
'Meditate upon your own 'Self' as that, which not only you desire,
but everyone else also desires.' Your 'Inner Self,' is the source of all
happiness, the happiness that one seeks here and there, all through
one's life. The *rishi* adds, 'Whoever knows it thus, all beings seek
Him.' If someone knows this, if someone has realized this truth,
then all others seek Him out, because everybody seeks happiness.
So if they get a hint that perhaps this person will provide what is
being sought, then 'all beings seek Him.' Everybody seeks bliss, but
this bliss must be experiential, it cannot be theoretical. At the theoretical level, one can discuss a hundred theories. It is like discussing
the art of swimming or cycling. It is good to discuss theory, but it
is useless without practice! Unless and until the discovery becomes
part of one's own experience and realization, it will remain a useless
theory.

Now the seventh *shloka* is interesting because it happens very
often. After all this teaching, the pupil tells the master:
'Sir, teach me the *Upanishad* – the secret of the *Upanishad.*'

SHLOKA 7

upanishadam bho bruhi iti uktaa ta upanishat
braahmeem vaava ta upanishadam abruma iti.

Upanishadam bho bruhi iti:
'It has already been taught! says the Master. 'The secret relating to *Brahman* has already been taught to you!' But apparently the student who sat through the whole discussion is not satisfied and says, 'Sir, please teach me the *Upanishad*.'

A certain great man was speaking to a group about *dhyana* – which is the practical part of the *Upanishad*. They heard him speak. They thought they were listening carefully to his discourse, but at the end of it, one among the group got up and said, 'But Sir, tell us about *dhyana*.' The speaker exclaimed, 'O god, what else have I been doing!'

This happens often. The reason is that one does not give enough attention to what is being said. The mind wanders, it alights on different things like a monkey and does not focus on reality. It likes to ruminate on past experience and speculate on the future. To have personal experience of the Supreme Being, what we require is absolute and total attention, as if one is listening to something for the first time. The moment one starts to compare and think, 'Has this been said before?' while one is supposedly listening to the Master, then one is not really listening to him at all! When one is listening, one must listen absolutely, with total attention, as if listening for the first time. This is because the knowledge of *Brahman* is something that should be known now, immediately. It is not as if, 'I will learn about it here, go home, think about it and decide whether to know *Brahman* or not!'

But this disciple, after listening to the whole thing says, 'Please teach me the *Upanishad*.' And the master replies, 'That I have already taught you.' This also means that whatever has been taught are only words. Since all the words have been listened to, and they remain only words, perhaps the pupil has been brought in to speak for us – 'We have heard the words, but what is the truth behind them? Can we make it our own, or is it just written in the *Upanishad*?' That is why the *Upanishad* is written in the form of a dialogue between the teacher and the disciple, to teach others having the same doubts. And the true master never gets fed up with a disciple, however little he understands at first.

There is this famous story about Shankaracharya's chief disciple, Hastaamalaka. When Shankaracharya was traveling in South India, he came to a village where the people brought to him a boy who had not spoken. They thought he was born dumb or retarded, and they thought that Shankaracharya being a great person, might be able to do something for him. Shankaracharya sat near him and asked, 'Why don't you speak?' And the boy spoke for the first time – 'About what? The Truth, the Reality cannot be put into words. So, why should I speak ?' He was called 'Hastaa-malaka' – 'he who had the wisdom of the Vedas in the form of an *amalaka* fruit, in his fist – *hasta*.' He became Shankaracharya's chief disciple.

When the pupil asked the master again, the master explained it again. So far, the explanation was too profound to understand. Now, the explanation is given in a practical manner.

SHLOKA 8

tasyaitapo dama karmeti pratishtha vedah
sarvaangani satyam aayatanam.

Tapah dama karma – austerity.' 'self-control' and 'work' – these are the supports, the foundation of *Brahman*, that 'Supreme Being' of which you ask again.

Tapah is usually interpreted as 'austerities.' If somebody takes a vow and stands with one hand upwards for ten years, well, some call it *tapas*. The word *tapas* is derived from the root *tap*, which means 'to burn.' So, *tapas* also means 'to burn away.' But austerity is not just having one loin cloth, or standing with one hand raised up!

There is this story about Janaka Maharaj who used to go to the forest to study at the feet of his master, the great sage Yagnavalkya, who always had a seat in front reserved for the king. The other ascetics and *sanyasins* used to feel jealous of the king. They thought that the Maharshi was either afraid of him or partial to him because he was a king. But Yagnavalkya said nothing, for generally, sages do not react to criticism!

One day, while the group was discussing the *Upanishads*, the truth of *Brahman*, the reality of existence and so on, a messenger came running, saying, 'Sir, *Videha* is burning and the fire is spreading into the forest!' Some of the ascetics started running to save their belongings from the fire – their clothes (*kaupin*) and their vessels (*kamandalu*). Only Janaka Maharaj kept seated and quiet.

The *Rishi* turned to the ascetics and said, 'This is the difference between him and you! His whole kingdom is burning but his attention is on *Brahman*, whereas you are running after your meagre possessions! You think you have given up the world but in reality you have not!'

You see, there is a great deal of difference between physically giving up and actually giving up. If one has given up all material possessions, yet is attached to what little one has, then one has not really given up! It is good to have a middle path with no extremes. Have what is necessary and have no craving for more. As Krishna says in the Gita, 'This *yoga* is not for him who eats too much or too little, or sleeps too much or too little'. There is a beautiful sentence in the *Ishavasya Upanishad,* which says, *tena tyaktena bhunjita* – 'let go and rejoice!' Normally when you let go, you suffer!

Once, when Swami Vivekananda was wandering around India, a young man came to him and said, 'Sir, I want to renounce everything and become a *sanyasin*.' Swamiji said, 'Great! You must be a mature man to be able to do that! What is your education?' The young man said that he had not completed his high school. Swamiji asked, 'What about your background?' The young man replied that his parents were dead. He had nothing, no home. Swamiji said, 'Then what are you going to renounce?' The young man said that he wanted to give up what little he had and become like the Buddha. And Swamiji replied, "Buddha had a whole kingdom to renounce, but you have nothing to let go! Go and make some money first, even if you have to steal! And when you have a lakh of rupees in your hand, you can come and say, 'Swamiji, I have this much; I am going to give it up and become a *sanyasin*,' and then I'll accept your request!"

Tapah is 'the burning away of the dross,' 'the burning away of one's accumulated impurities' or 'distractions.' Once one begins to understand that the 'Inner Self,' the 'Supreme Being' is not touched by any of the ups and downs of the world and its emotions, one has become a little richer. Slowly, the disturbances begin to subside. Ultimately, the burning away of the ego takes place. In Dakshineshwar, you will see Kali with a garland of human heads. When one is ready to give one's head as part of the garland, then one has burnt everything off! That is real *tapas*.

So, what are the supports of *Brahman*? They are *tapas, dama* and *karma* or 'austerity,' 'self-control' and 'work.' 'Giving-up' and 'burning-down' is *tapas*, not becoming lazy. There is a great deal of difference between *satva* and *tamo guna*. In *satva*, there is goodness and purity. One finds no reason to do anything. In laziness, one does not *want* to do anything at all. That is the difference.

The study of the *Upanishads* is a great effort. Working towards a great goal requires great effort. *Karma* here means 'the work towards the attainment of the Supreme Being,' putting great effort to acquire the knowledge of the Supreme Being. *Dama* means 'self control,' which means not letting the mind take control of you. The mind is not allowed to dictate to you. You dictate what the mind should do, so that it is no more dissipated, it is no more running here and there like a monkey. It is calm, settled and quiet. So, *tapas, dama* and *karma* are the foundation for knowing *Brahman*.

Another important statement is made – *vedah sarvaangani* – 'the Vedas are its units.' The *Vedas,* which we study, are all units of the Supreme Being because they describe the different approaches, the different angles and different visions of looking at the Supreme Being.

The final statement is *satyam aayatanam*: 'Truth is its final abode.' To find this *satyam,* first one has to be free of all the *asatyam* which one has so long imagined to be true. Swami Vivekananda put this very aptly. He said, 'We have been hypnotized by *maya* ; now we have to dehypnotize ourselves.' When you get out of the abode of *asatyam,* you reach the abode of 'Truth' – *aayatanam satyam, satyam aayatanam.*

In various *Upanishads,* the states of *satyam* and *asatyam* have been described and compared to a dream. Suppose you have a lengthy dream in which you see yourself as a happy child sitting inside a marriage *pandal.* Suddenly the marriage *pandal* catches fire, and you, the child, are burnt! You wake up and say, 'Thank God that was a bad dream! I am fine in my own room!' In the dream state, you thought that it was the truth, but when you awoke, it was not. The waking state is the state of *satyam,* which is the reality of this world. But please note, even this worldly reality is only for the time being. You will find that, that is also *asatyam,* not the truth.

So, this realization of *Brahman* is like waking up from all dreams. When one has woken up from all the dreams, one says, 'Oh, what a long dream I had; what a long and lifelike dream! All the joys and sorrows of that dream state are over. Now, I am in the abode of 'Truth,' which is *Sat Chit Ananda* or, as Vyasa calls it in the Brahma Sutras – *Asti Bhati Priya.*

SHLOKA 9

*yo va etam evam veda apahatya paapmaanam ante svarge loke jyeye
pratitishtati pratitishtati*

'Whoever has known this, overcomes all sin in the end, and is
firmly established in the Supreme Consciousness, in the supreme
world of *svarga*.' Here, *svargaloka* is not the *svarga* which is described in the Puranas, where one enjoys oneself with rich food
and drink, lolling in a super-sized bed! Here it means the supreme
condition of total *moksha*, total freedom. And then, the *Upanishad*
emphasises, 'He is firmly established; he is firmly established in the
Truth' – *pratitishtati pratitishtati*.

With this, the *Kenopanishad* ends.

QUESTIONS AND ANSWERS

Q1.: *Other than Shankara's Vedanta, are there explanations which are
more satisfying, because devotion cannot go easily towards a formless
Being...*
A: Apart from Shankara's *Vedanta*, there are beautiful commentar-
ies written on all the *Upanishads* by Madhva. There are so many
Upanishads that talk about the *Brahman*. The approach of the
Kenopanishad is not the only exclusive approach to 'Reality.' *Isha
vaasyam idam sarvam*: everything is *Brahman*.

One is reminded of what Mahendranath Gupta said to Sri
Ramakrishna when they first met. Sri Ramakrishna asked
Mahendranath in his usual simple way, 'Do you believe in God
with form or without form?' Mahendranath straightaway went into
a lecture, 'All these clay and stone images ... these are all nonsense!
As you know the Supreme *Brahman* is ...' Sri Ramakrishna cut him
short and said, 'This is one hobby of you Calcutta people – you like

to lecture! If you believe that the Supreme *Brahman* is everywhere, that he is infinite, then why can't he be in an image? Why do you exclude the image?'

So, these are different approaches. One has to choose the explanation one is most comfortable with.

Q2.: *Since 'Truth' is one, is there the same interpretation in Islam, of* Brahman, *as in the Kenopanishad?*

A: The *Koran* has the stature of *Shruti*. Everything else, including *Hadis*, is considered to be a revelation; the *Hadis* comprises the sayings of Prophet Mohammad. In various places in the *Koran*, you find references to the Supreme Being in different ways. In some places the Supreme Being is represented as the creator, like Brahma. He creates, He destroys, He punishes; the Supreme Being becomes a God of the *saguna* variety. The God of the *Koran* is without form. He has no *roopa*, but He has qualities and attributes. So, what would you call Him? *Niraakaar* or *niraakaar saguna* because the *gunas* are there.

There are some places where there is mention of God from whom both good and evil have started. This kind of mention is very rare. There is one stream of Islam called the *Sufi* stream, followed by those who have gone into the mystical aspect of the religion. They are not so much concerned with what is called *Shariat*, but they discuss the *Tariqat*. Unfortunately, *Sufis* are prohibited from entering many Islamic countries. India is one country where Sufis have never been persecuted. One of the greatest Sufis, Ali Mansoor Al Halaj, was executed in Baghdad for proclaiming *'Anul Haq'* – 'I am the Truth!' In the *Sufi* stream, there is also mention of *Brahman*, which has been described in the Kenopanishad.

'*Sufi*' is a word coined by some European writers on Islam. The Sufi himself does not know that he is called a '*Sufi*'! They generally like to call themselves 'people on the path' or 'travelers.' The whole *Sufi* system is built on a personal saying of Mohammad which is called 'Hadis' – *Man arfa nafsu fa khad arfa rabbu* – which means, 'He who knows his Self knoweth his Lord.' The entire *Sufi* system has been built on this. So, considering it that way, *Brahman*, as referred to in the Kenopanishad, also exists, especially with the *Sufis*. But in the rest of the *Koran* you will find the *saguna Brahman* generally, God as creator, God as preserver, God as destroyer, God without form but with attributes. In a few rare places, the Supreme Reality is referred to as the 'Light that shines like a lamp in the *khalb* – heart.'

Q3.: *What is the difference between Gods such as Sri Rama and Sri Krishna and the Supreme Brahman? Where are these gods? How is it that when we pray we get God's blessings? We also have a feeling that a kind of power exists at some particular place, at Vaishno Devi, for instance. What are these powers?*

A: It must be made clear that nowhere do the *Upanishads* declare that there are no gods or there are no powers of nature or there are no higher beings. In this *Upanishad* itself one finds many references to gods, higher powers of nature to whom one prays and gets help. But what the *Upanishads* say is that the Core or the Essence of even those gods is the Supreme Being. This is what this *Upanishad* declares – that even the gods derive their power from that Supreme Being.

When one prays, does one get blessings? Somtimes one does and sometimes one does not. It depends not only on how much one prays or what energy one puts into it; it also depends on the circumstances. Often we pray for things that we want, but they may not be the things we need for our evolution. There is a difference between what you want and what you need to evolve spiritually. Since the Supreme Being is concerned with your need to evolve rather than satisfy your want at that moment, sometimes prayers are not answered. But the mind has such powers that if you apply your mind to achieving something, ninety-nine percent, we must always leave one percent to chance, you will get it. One must know how to get it, how to apply the mind. That is the whole science of *dhyana, dharana* and *samadhi.*

The *Tantra Shastras* not only apply to higher things, they also apply to the achievement and attainment of things of this world. There are *havans*, there are *homas* and there are *pujas*. All these are there as forms of prayer. It so happens that the *Upanishads* do not deal with this, they deal with the Essence. However, they do not deny these forms of prayer. But for the seeker who is looking for the absolute, original, uncorrupted 'Truth', these are of no importance. That is all that is said.

About places like Vaishno Devi, for instance, it is true that certain places acquire certain vibrations because of the presence of very highly evolved spiritual beings. Added to that are the concentrated energies of the hundreds and millions of people who visit the place, pray, and further strengthen the energies there.

When a temple is built, there is a process called *praana pratishta*. Before the *praana pratishta* is done, the image is nothing. The sculptor might sit on the head of *Vishnu* and knock at the nose as he carves the stone, because it has not become *Vishnu* yet. Once the image is installed, when the *praana pratishta* is done, the stone idol becomes God!

The process of *praana pratishta*, apart from the *mantras* and rituals, is very interesting. The person who does the *praana pratishta* first visualizes the cavern of his heart as well lit and clean. Then he does what is called *aavaahan*, which means he invites the God to be present in his heart. When he has brought the God into his heart, then he does the *pratishta*. He passes the God on to the image and says, 'Please enter this image so that we may pray to you from here.' Once the *prana pratishta* is done, it becomes powerful, and then, depending on the performance of the daily rituals and the attention given by the hundreds of people who go there, it becomes more and more powerful. The power is provided from within, but it can also come from without.

There are some special places where there are special vibrations. People are now studying the effect of pyramids, for example. The *Upanishads* do not talk about it, but it does not mean that they do not exist. It is just that the *Upanishads* are concerned with something different.

Q4.: *In this* Upanishad, *when* Vayu, Agni *and* Indra *could not understand the Inner Being, the* Para Brahman, *who is this* Uma *that makes you understand?*
A: The question is, 'Who is Uma?' Uma is always associated with *Shiva-Parvati*; Uma is the mystical energy that is in all of us which has been variously referred to as the *Kundalini*. When that energy is aroused and made active, then different instruments of perception come into being. Among those instruments, the most important is the center called the *Ajna Chakra*, which is again represented in *Shiva* as the third eye. This is why Shiva is called *Trayambak* – 'the one with three eyes.' It is that eye, the single eye, which when opens, your whole being is full of light. There is a statement in the New Testament: 'Therefore, if thine eye be single, thy whole body shall be full of light!' Obviously, it does not refer to being blind in one eye!

So, this Uma within, when considered as an internal force, is that energy, or *Shakti*, or *Kundalini*, which opens up one's wisdom and takes one to the *Brahman*, the Supreme Reality.

Q5.: *Quite often,* moha – *love, attraction, worldly ties* – *stops one from letting 'the breeze' blow in. Can you help?*
A: Yes, there is a dilemma here. There is no way out except to find out the cause of *moha*, how it can be controlled, and then control it. We teachers can help in a limited way, but ultimately, the work has to be done by the person himself. If help in personal *sadhana* is required, then one has to meet individually and discuss it because there is no single path or method that is suitable for everyone. Each person has a different background, a different mindset and is ge-

netically different. So, one has to have *satsang*, which means one has to sit down and talk and listen. This is what happened during the *Upanishadic* period, where the teacher and the student talked and tried to understand each other and explored ways to find out how to overcome the problem. That sort of help, or association, can be provided by the teacher.

Q6.: *What is the middle point between* moha *and* moksha?
A: It depends on how serious and how evolved the person asking the question is. If the person is keen on *moksha*, or salvation then he is at the stage when he is really keen to get rid of *moha* or lust and attraction to material things, and he wants to get over it and achieve *moksha*. On the other hand, if he is not keen to achieve *moksha*, there is little purpose in an answer, is it not? In any case, that person is definitely caught between the pulls of *moha* and the search for *moksha*. He wants to attain *moksha*, for which he has to overcome *moha*.

One cannot define a mid-point between the two. It depends on each individual and how much he aspires for *moksha*. There are several people who want to get *moksha*, but they are so caught up in the web of their *mohas* that they cannot. They find it too difficult. Yet it is better to be in that state than not to even think of *moksha*. When you say you wish to overcome *moha*, it means you have understood that there is a problem with *moha*. That is a positive step. It is actually the state of a seeker, a *jijnasu*, and it is an important step because from there one moves forward.

Q7.: *Why couldn't the young man who spoke to Swami Vivekananda say that he wanted to renounce his ignorance and not material things?*
A: One does not know the mental state of the young man when he came up with such a question! If he had said, 'I want to renounce my ignorance,' Swamiji would have probably asked him to get ready and begin to understand because ignorance goes only when knowledge comes in.

Q8.: *Could you please tell us something about the Gayatri Mantra? Can it be recited at night time as well?*

A: The *Gayatri Mantra* is the essence of the *Vedas*. The *Mantra* is:

> *om bhur bhuva suvah*
> *tat savitur varenyam*
> *bhargo devasya dheemahi*
> *dhiyo yonah prachodayaat*

If one could explain *Om* and *bhur bhuva suvah*, we have explained the entire *Vedanta*. That is why it is called the Essence of the *Vedas*! Although it is not the intention here to explain the whole of the *Gayatri*, one can say that the reason the *Gayatri* is chanted is to clear your intellect and make it subtle enough to understand the higher mysteries of life.

The other reason is that the regular chanting of the *Gayatri* definitely builds up a certain vibration which is very conducive to spiritual as well as material welfare. This is a personal experience. Perhaps one of the reasons why there is a downfall in the moral calibre of this country is because those who are given the *Gayatri* and asked to chant it have stopped doing so!

Those who can see invisible things, who are clairvoyants, have actually seen certain vibrations taking place when one chants the *Gayatri* properly, even if one does not know the meaning. The effect of the chanting is that it not only emanates from the person who is chanting, it goes through the people who are listening as well. This is because the words and the rhythm have been set in such a fashion.

Now the question – 'can it be recited at night as well?' Normally, the *Gayatri* is not chanted at night simply because it is a *mantra* which is a request to the Sun god to illumine the intellect. It is also chanted facing the Sun. But, for *sadhaks* who believe that the Sun which they address is the inner Sun of knowledge and illumination – with that attitude, perhaps, one can chant the *Gayatri* even at night. The *Savitur* need not be only the physical manifestation, it can be the inner Sun which gives wisdom and light. Therefore, if one thinks of it in that way, there should be no bar in chanting the *Gayatri* at any time.

Again, *Gayatri* need not be chanted loudly. It can be chanted mentally. Indeed, it is mostly chanted quietly. Even when the *Gayatri* is given to somebody, it is whispered in the ear.

Q9.: *Is there any reference to* Purusha *and* Prakriti *in any* Upanishad? *If there is, then where does* Brahman *stand in that scheme?*

A: *Purusha* has been referred to in the *Vedas* – for instance, in the *Rig Veda*, there is the *Purusha Suktam* – but *Prakriti* is not referred to directly in the *Upanishads*. *Purusha* and *Prakriti*, as such, are mainly referred to in the *Sankhya Sutras* of Kapila. In the *Sankhya Pravanchana Sutra*, for instance, *Prakriti* has been given a definition. It says, *prakaroti iti prakriti* – that means, 'that which divides, that which creates duality, which creates division, is *Prakriti*' and, *Purusha* is the unified power from which *Prakriti* emanates. In the *Upanishads*, there is reference to *Purusha*. In the *Purusha Suktam* of the *Rig Veda*, the Supreme Being is called *Purusha*, who is *sahasraaksha*, 'He who has a thousand eyes.' *Sahasra* does not necessarily mean 'one thousand.' The reference here is to the Supreme Divine Being who can see everything and is aware of everything. He is Omnipresent, Omnipotent and Omniscient. According to the *Upanishads* and the Vedas, *Purusha* is often a substitute word for the *Brahman*, the 'Supreme Being.'

'That *Purusha* also resides in oneself.' In this context, it refers to the 'Self' and the 'Self' is the *atman*; the *atman* and the *Brahman* are the same, or at least, linked together. So, the reference to the *Purusha* in the *Vedas* and the *Upanishads* is actually a reference to the *Brahman*.

Q10.: *After all this discussion on* Brahman, *you have said that one should experience one's 'Self.' How is this brought about and what is the place of the teacher in this regard?*

A: This is a serious question. We have had so much discussion on the *Brahman*, but will it remain only at the theoretical level, the academic level, or the verbal level? Can one really experience this, which we are talking about? And, if we can, what is the role of the teacher in this search?

The guide or the teacher is the one who points the way. He says, 'This is the way you have to take – now, follow it.' To find out and to experiment with the methods given by the teacher, is the job of the seeker. The teacher cannot work for the seeker. He can be a catalyst, but the actual experience has to be gained by the seeker himself.

For instance, suppose you are standing at a junction and a man comes up to you and asks, 'Sir, where is this address I am looking for? How do I get there?' You say, 'Go straight, turn left ... that is the building.' Now, what should he do? Should he proceed along the way shown to him? Or should he stay back and garland you saying, 'Sir, you are the greatest teacher. You have shown me the way. Now I know all that I want to know.'

The function of the teacher is to show the way, and once the path is shown, the seeker should get ready to move on the path and not stay with the teacher. A true teacher would not like to be praised or flattered. He should say, 'If you want the truth, do what I have asked you to do; perform what I have asked you to perform.'

In the *Vedas*, the *Upanishads* and the *Agamas*, the word for teacher is *Guru*. It is derived from *gu* and *ru*. *Ru* meaning *Rudra*, 'the destroyer' of *gu*, meaning darkness or the hidden. So, 'One who destroys the darkness' or 'One who brings out what is hidden' or 'One who reveals the Truth.'

In *Vedantic* parlance, a *Guru* can be best illustrated by an example. It seems there were eleven people who went on an excursion. They crossed a stream, and when they reached the other side, they suddenly had a doubt whether anybody had been left behind. One person stood up and started counting. He counted and said, 'There are only ten people here. There is one chap missing.' Then another person in the group said, 'This cannot be! I can see everybody here.' Then he too counted and said, 'It's true! There are only ten! Who is missing?' While this circus was going on, a person who had climbed a palm tree to tap toddy was watching them. He came down and said, 'Don't worry! I have counted. You are eleven.' The chap who counted everybody, forgot to count himself! The toddy-tapper is the *Guru*, you see, because he looked at the situation from a totally different point of view, reassured and corrected the perception of the group. He only made them aware. For that, a teacher was essential. This, in *Vedantic* terms, is the function of the teacher.

Q11.: *Is it by accident that the teacher appears in front of you?*
A: Well, what we call 'accidents' are things about which we are not aware, about which we do not know. Let us say there is a giant jigsaw puzzle; and the person who makes the jigsaw puzzle, the one who draws the picture and paints it and then cuts it up into little pieces – he knows what the ultimate figure looks like. Suppose the pieces of the jigsaw puzzle are taken apart and the different pieces lie here and there. I pick up one piece in isolation. I see that it does not even have a regular geometrical shape, and say, 'This is meaningless. What is this?' If I can put all the pieces together, then I see that there is some meaning to it. And the one who has made the jigsaw puzzle knows what it is. If one is to find out the meaning of the jigsaw puzzle one has to have the same angle of vision as the creator of the jigsaw puzzle. I must be like the toddy-tapper, who stood outside and saw who was missing.

When a person is ready for his spiritual progress, then the teacher definitely appears. It need not be one teacher. The *Avadhoot* had twenty four teachers. Even the bee was his teacher. There can be many teachers, but generally there is one person who is the guide. The only thing that one has to be very careful about is the choice of the guide. Of course, when one is ready, one will get the teacher. How and why does the teacher pick his student or the student pick his teacher? There is always a reason, though it is not known at the time!

One does not have to run to the Himalayas in search of a *Guru*. One may do so out of great enthusiasm, but it is not necessary. One is drawn to the teacher at the right moment. The teacher will come – definitely! It has always happened that when the aspirant is ready, the teacher has always appeared. Either he goes to the teacher, or the teacher goes to him. It is no accident.

Om Shantih! Om Shantih! Om Shantih!

Mandukya Upanishad

he *Upanishads* form part of the *Vedas*. When we talk about the *Vedas*, it is generally the *Samhita* portions; *Samhita*, meaning, 'the hymns' of the *Vedas*, which are the *Rig Veda*, the *Yajur Veda*, the *Sama Veda* and the *Atharvana Veda*. These are the four important *Vedas* that have been handed down to us from time immemorial. In fact, no one can say where they originated or how they came to us. They are known as *shruti* because it is said that they were 'heard.' *Shruti* means 'through the ear.' *Shruti* was heard by the wise *rishis* of ancient times who passed down the body of wisdom that takes us to the essence of all life and provides the answers to questions like – What is God? What is the human being? How is human life connected to God? And so on and so forth.

The last portion of the *Vedas* is a section that is known as the *Jnana Kanda*, which means 'the Wisdom Section.' This is the section where the *Upanishads* come in. So they are basically discussions on the truths which have been given in the *shruti*. The *Upanishads* themselves are considered to be *shruti*. They bring us to an understanding, first theoretically and then actually, of what we call the 'Supreme Being,' *Brahman* or *Atman* or *Ishwara*.

Now, the meaning of the word 'Upanishad' – *Upa* means 'to move closer,' 'to go nearer' and *shad* means 'to sit down' physically and also to settle down the mind. Two interpretations have been given: The first is, 'to sit in front of the teacher.' You can imagine the situation in ancient times where there would be a beautiful hermitage on the banks of a river beside the mountains, where the great *rishi* taught his students who sat around him. The students did not sit far away, so there was always a personal contact with the students. These are matters where personal contact is very important. So, the teacher and the students sat down close to each other, and the students listened to the truths that were being expounded by the teacher.

There is the syllable *ni* that connects *upa* and *shad*. *Ni* indicates the level at which the person who 'receives' sits – a little 'lower' than the teacher. It does not mean the physical level. It indicates a psychological state of mind, where the disciple or the seeker acknowledges that he does not know. He supposes that his teacher, the *rishi*, knows, and therefore he sits down with humility. This is the meaning of *ni* – 'to sit down at a lower level with great humility.' He sits down and listens to the teacher propounding the truths of the *shruti* and explaining them. This is the meaning of 'Upanishad.'

When you say *shad*, 'to sit,' it means not only to physically sit down but it also means 'the settling down of the mind' which normally is attracted by all the activities of the material world and runs hither and thither like a monkey all the time. We must understand that the teaching of the *Upanishad*, specifically, is meant for those who have already gone through certain *sadhanas* and have acquired the capacity, relatively speaking, to still their minds and sit. They would have also acquired the humility to know that they do not know and are ready to listen. So, when all these activities come together, they form the subject matter of the *Upanishads*.

One important point is that the *Upanishads* are often in the form of a dialogue between the teacher and the disciple, and they are profoundly clear after explanation. But somewhere along the line there has come about a misunderstanding that, since the *Upanishads* are in the *Jnana Kanda* or the intellectual part of the scriptures, one can find the truth, which the *Upanishads* express, through intellectual acrobatics. We must understand very clearly that the *Upanishads* do not claim or state that one can find the 'Supreme Reality' through intellectual analysis. Intellectual analysis is very necessary, the intellect is very important, but nowhere do the *Upanishads* say that through the workings of the brain alone can one find the 'Supreme Being.' In fact, the entire purport of the *Upanishads* is to make one understand that there is 'something' which is beyond the thinking brain, beyond the intellect, something which is much wider and larger in scope than our limited brain can comprehend.

The *Upanishads* tell us how to open up the channels of communion with the Supreme. Many people think that the study of the *Upanishads* is an intellectual exercise. There are people who think that if you study the *Upanishads*, you will find God immediately. That is not true. In fact, by use of the intellect alone one cannot reach the 'Supreme Being.'

The *Kena Upanishad*, one of the *Upanishads* of the *Sama Veda*, declares in unequivocal terms that, 'That Supreme Being which you are seeking cannot be reached even by the mind.' By 'mind' is meant our normal mind, which logically concludes, 'one plus one is two,' and so on. Seeking the 'Supreme Being' is something that comes about when the mind has completely settled down; when it has understood that no amount of intellectual acrobatics is going to solve the problem. When the mind is in peace, then, actually, begins the journey. The *Upanishads* bring us to the beginnning of the journey.

The *Kena Upanishad* says:
yan manasaa na manute yena ahur mano matam
tadeva brahma tvam viddhi nedam yad idam upaasate.

Yan manasaa na manute – 'That which the mind cannot conceive.'

Yen ahur mano matum – 'But because of which the mind gets the capacity to function.'

Tad eva brahma tvam viddhi – 'Understand that 'That' is the Supreme Being.'

Nedam yad idam upaasate – 'Nothing that you consider here.'

It means that you can formulate nothing with your brain which can, in any way, describe that 'Supreme being' who is the very origin of the mind.

Sometimes, when one learns the *Upanishads* and other such scriptures, one is filled with a subtle egotism, 'Now that I have read all this, I have understood the Supreme Being.' This is far from the truth. If that were so, then no *sadhana* would have been prescribed. These are the two important points – one is the intellectual understanding and the other is *sadhana,* which one has to practise after learning personally from a teacher. Even the great Shankaracharya who had said *'jagat mithya,'* still prescribed *sadhana,* because without *sadhana* we can understand very little.

One has to listen to the *Upanishads* carefully, for much of our thinking and understanding is prejudiced. We are so caught up in the attraction of the world and our senses that though we think that we think clearly, our thinking is, in fact, always prejudiced by our desires. So, we have to watch our mind and proceed carefully.

The *Mandukya Upanishad* is a short *Upanishad.* It consists of just twelve verses or *shlokas.* Gaudapada has written a voluminous *karika,* or commentary on it. All the great *acharyas,* including Shankaracharya, Madhvacharya and Ramanuja, have written commentaries on it.

It is a short *Upanishad* which deals with the subject that is so basic to our living and our understanding of life. It is called *'Mandukya Upanishad'* because according to tradition, *Varun Dev, the lord of the rains,* took the form of a *manduka,* a frog, and taught this *Upanishad* as *Mandukya Maharshi.*

Manduka actually means 'frog.' Normally when we look at a frog, we think that it is a useless, insignificant little creature; it may even look funny or repulsive to us. The frog may be insignificant to us, but, when wisdom comes through the mouth of a frog, its external appearance is no longer important. Maturity and inner wisdom are more important than outward appearances.

Another point is that the frog, lone among all creatures that we know of, passes through quite a metamorphosis through a cycle where it emerges from the egg, becomes a tadpole that swims around in the water, and discards its tail to become a frog. Then it begins to live both on land and in water. It is a great transformation that takes place. This is the first metamorphosis which we are taught in school. It is also, in some way, a reference to a spiritually advanced being or a *rishi* who in his complete spiritual understanding, has 'discarded his tail.' Like a frog that can live both in water and on land, a *rishi* is in two worlds at the same time – the material and the spiritual.

If you have read some of the discussions in the books on Sri Ramakrishna Paramahamsa, you will find an interesting incident mentioned. Sri Ramakrishna once said, 'I am going to Calcutta. Though I don't meet many people there, I will meet Keshab Chandra Sen.' When he met Keshab Chandra Sen, he said, 'Do you know why I have come to meet you? Not because you are the founder of the Brahmo Samaj, but because you are one of the few people whose tail has been discarded!' Everybody wondered what 'tail' he was talking about. Remember, only when the tadpole's tail is discarded does it becomes a full-fledged frog. So what he meant was, 'You are no longer a tadpole, you are fully grown and can live in two worlds – here and there at the same time.'

Live in the world of the spirit, anchored in the world of the spirit, and yet carry on in this world. A beautiful example is that of the lotus, which grows in the water, taking all its sustenance from the mud underneath, yet not a drop of water will stick to its petals. So also, derive all your sustenance from the world, and yet remain unaffected by it. Some people think that it is not possible. One has to try!

If one remains trapped by the attractions of this world, it means one is not trying hard enough, and if that be so, it only means that one's priorities are not yet decided – that is all. People have this approach – 'We will work hard for anything,' – for instance, a promotion or a fat bank balance, 'but where spiritual development is concerned, a short-cut would be nice!'

No *Upanishad*, no religious teacher has said that we must renounce the world and live in isolation. It is so difficult in this *Kaliyuga* for a person to go away, sit in a cave and meditate. It is impossible because we carry our mind with us; we are not free from the mind which comes with us wherever we go. Even if we do go away, how do we find out whether we have progressed spiritually, sitting alone out there? Suppose one lives in isolation for three months and feels one has conquered anger. How can one know it as a fact? There is nobody to get angry with out there, except the walls of the cave. It is only when one comes out of the 'cave' and tries to get into a crowded bus and somebody gives him a painful shove, can one know whether one is really free of anger or not! So, these things can be tested only in society, in the midst of people.

Of course, when one has performed all one's life's work and discharged one's responsibilities, then one is free to go. But there is no point in running away prematurely, for trivial reasons. That is what is called 'the *vairagya* of the monkey.' I get upset with my wife, we have a big quarrel; so I renounce everything and go off to Benaras. This is not *vairagya*! *Vairagya* is something that comes from within after a great deal of introspection and maturity, and is very rare. One has to be very mature to be free; then one can physically go away somewhere. For most of us the ideal thing would be to live here and also to understand.

As was said in the beginning, the *Upanishads* are part of the *Rig, Yajur, Sama* and *Atharvana Vedas*. The *Mandukya Upanishad* belongs to the *Atharvana Veda*, the last of the four *Vedas*. It deals basically with the significance of *aum*. It begins with the description of what *aum* is, and then goes on to describe the basic experience of all human beings, irrespective of their caste, creed or religion.

The basic experience all human beings have is that we are awake, we all dream, and we have deep sleep. These three states of consciousness and how they are connected with *aum* is the subject matter of this Upanishad. It has only twelve *shlokas*. Yet, hundreds of pages have been written discussing these twelve *shlokas*.

SHLOKA 1

aum ity etad aksharam idam sarvam tasyopa vyaakhyaanam
bhutam bhavad bhavishyaditi sarvam aumkaara eva
yacchaanyat trikaalaateetam tad apy aumkaara eva.

Aum ity etad – The sound *aum*, 'this syllable.'

Aksharam – 'indestructible,' that which remains forever. *Kshara* means, 'that which can be destroyed' and *akshara* means 'that which cannot be destroyed.' It also means 'that which cannot be born,' because anything which is born is destroyed at some point. *Aum* is 'unborn,' 'forever, 'eternal,' 'ever-existing.'

Idam sarvam – 'That is all This,' which means, nothing can be ruled out from the field of aum; everything is within its purview. 'That indestructible *akshara* is everything.'

To make us understand this statement, it has to be interpreted. So, the teacher says, *tasyopa vyaakhyaanam* – 'I am giving a commentary on this to make you understand what is meant by, 'it is *aksharam*' and 'it is *idam sarvam*.'

Bhutam bhavad bhavishyaditi – 'It is all that is past, present and future.' All that existed, exists and is going to exist, *sarvam omkaara eva* – 'All this is only *aum*.' That Supreme sound, *aum*, is all that was, is and will be. That is the *aum*, which is the subject matter of discussion of this *Upanishad*.

So, *aum* is time – past, present and future. There is something interesting here to note: as far as the human mind is concerned, the past is something which exists only in the form of a memory – it does not exist in reality anymore. When you say, 'Yesterday I did such and such a thing,' the act is over, finished, there is nothing left of it. What I can see is only the present reality. The future I cannot see, I can only speculate. This is the limitation of the human mind. It cannot live in the past, the present, and the future at the same time! It can think of the past, but thinking of the past is not living in the past. It is only a mental process, a memory.

The only thing one is sure of, is the present. One is not sure of the future because it is speculation. Based on the past, through the present, one speculates on what the future could hold. One can only project the present into the future and say, 'This is what could be;' which may or may not be. The only certainty that the human being can experience is the present. And every second, every moment of the present is going into the past. One says, 'I am going to think of something ...' and the moment I have thought about it, I store it in my memory. It has gone into the past! All of us live in this flow of the past through the present and into the future. This is the movement through which we live, and this is what gives us hope.

Now, the 'Supreme Being' who is mentioned in the *Upanishad*, this *aum* is, *bhutam bhavad bhavishyad iti sarvam*: 'It is the past, the present and the future', all together at the same time! *Sarvam* – everything is included in it. It is something outside the limited scope of our comprehension – the past, the present and the future, all together, at the same time!

Normally, when we say 'past,' we think of something that happened before, and when we think of the future, we think of something that is going to happen later. As for the Supreme *aum*, what has happened, what is happening and and what is going to happen is all known at the same time! We cannot conceive of such a situation. The human mind is simply incapable of it! We can only think of life and experience in terms of past, present and future.

But the rishi of the *Mandukya Upanishad* says, *Yacchaanyat tri-kaalaateetam tad apy aumkaara eva* – there exists something which is beyond the *trikaala* – beyond the past, present and future, all that is *aumkaara*. There is nothing beyond *aumkaara*. *Aum* represents the 'Supreme Being.' The Supreme Brahman of the *Upanishad* is represented here and explained as – 'that which is beyond the past, present and the future.' As explained earlier, it is much beyond the capacity of the mind to think of 'that' which is beyond the past, present and future. We cannot conceive of this because all our experiences are based on the passage of time.

On the one hand, it shows how insignificant we are. On the other hand, it tells us that since we are a spark of that 'Supreme Being,' we are really significant! It is both ways!

Any *Upanishad* can be understood only after one has gone through a certain degree of *sadhana*. Without that, certain parts of it may appear a little too abstract. We must go into it carefully, slowly with mental preparation, and then try to understand.

Then the *rishi* confirms what has been said before:

SHLOKA 2

sarvam hyetad brahma ayam atmaa brahma
soyam atmaa chatushpaad

Sarvam hyetad brahma – 'All this is verily *Brahman*.' There is nothing that is not *Brahman*, meaning, there is nothing that can be taken out and said, 'This is not *Brahman*; this is separate from *Brahman*,' because everything is included in that: past, present, future and that which is beyond past, present and future. Everything is included in this 'Supreme Being' who is expressed here as *aum*.

The next sentence is one of the *Mahavakyas*. It has been variously interpreted.

Ayam atma brahma: 'This Self is *Brahman*.' 'Self' is not to be interpreted as 'the limited self.' 'This Self ' means the *atma*, which is not an abstract 'something' but real living consciousness.

We are not talking about an energy, like chemical energy or atomic energy, which does not have an intelligence of its own. We are talking about an intelligent energy; we are talking about an intelligent 'Being.' That very word, *'atma'* is used here to denote that we are not talking about an abstraction or a state of mind. We are talking about a 'Being.' Only a 'Being' has *atman*. An inanimate object does not have an *atman*.

So, this 'Being,' the *aumkara*, the *Brahman*, is not an abstract 'something' hanging in the air. It is not merely an idea. Somebody said that 'God is a state of mind.' God is not simply 'state of mind.' Probably in a certain state of mind one can have close communion with God – that is understandable. But a statement that 'God is a state of mind' is limited in its understanding . So, first the *rishi* says, *Sarvam hy etad brahma* – 'All this is verily that

Brahman.' And then he says, *Ayam atmaa brahma* – 'This *atma* is *Brahman.*' That Supreme Reality, *Brahman*, is *atma*, which means, 'It' is a Conscious Being and not an abstract idea.

Soyam atma chatushpaad – and this *atma*, this 'Self,' this real living 'Being,' who is beyond the past, the present and the future, has 'four parts' – *chatushpaad*. We will study the four parts and see how they are connected with the word *aum*.

Aum is divided into three syllables 'A' 'U' 'M.' One interpretation of *aum* is that 'A' represents the beginning of creation, 'U' represents preservation of that which has been created and 'M' represents the end of creation. So, *aum* is interpreted as creation, preservation and destruction. Actually, we must not call it 'destruction' but 'regeneration,' because only when the old is destroyed does the new come up!

In this *Upanishad*, however, *aum* symbolizes the different states of our consciousness: the waking state, the dream state and the deep-sleep state. All of us experience these uniformly. This is something we cannot deny. We are awake, we dream and we sleep. This is common to all human beings.

The *Mandukya Upanishad* identifies the sound 'A' with the 'waking state' – *jagrita avastha*; 'U' with the 'dream state' – *swapna avastha*; and 'M' with 'deep sleep' – *sushupti*.

In addition to the three syllables of *aum* – 'A,' 'U' and 'M,' we have the *ardha matra*. This is the sound that comes after *aum* has been chanted. When we say aum, that last '... mmm ...' is the *ardha matra*. The verse that follows is a description about that.

SHLOKA 3

jagrita sthaano bahish prajnah saptaanga
ekonavimshati mukhah sthula bhug vaishwanarah prathamah paadah.

The first quarter of the four parts of that 'Supreme Reality,' the *Brahman*, is the *jagrita sthaan*. Its sphere of activity is the 'waking state' – *jagrita*. That means all of us who are awake are functioning because of the first quarter of that 'Supreme Being.' Without that, we will not be conscious of our waking state. The very consciousness and recognition that 'we are awake' is the first quarter of that 'Supreme Reality,' *Brahman*. The *jagrita* is its sphere of activity. And what is the sphere of activity in the waking state? How do we recognize that we are awake? We recognize objects, we see things, we hear, we taste, we are in contact with the world. That is the *jagrita avastha* – the state of wakefulness. So, the first quarter of that Supreme *Brahman*, that *atman* which we have described, is the 'waking state.'

It functions in the waking state of all human beings and in the actualities of their every day experiences. And its function is 'to recognize, to understand, to have knowledge of external objects' – *bahish prajnah*.

This part of that 'Supreme Being' causes the waking state and facilitates the recognition of external objects. Such a 'Supreme Being' has *saptaanga* – 'seven limbs.' This is a description of the *Purusha*, the 'Supreme Being', as represented in the *Agni Hotra*. It is the visualization of that 'Supreme Being' as a Super-person. It is a symbolic description of the Supreme Being as in the Chandogya Upanishad, 'That, whose head is the heavens; whose eyes are the sun; whose *praana* (life breath) is the air; whose middle portion is the mind; whose bladder is the waters of the earth; whose two feet are the earth, whose mouth is the fire of the *Agni Hotra*.' This is a symbolic representation and, relating to that symbol, the *rishi* says that It has 'seven limbs' – seven *angaas* including fire, which is symbolized as the mouth of that 'Supreme Being.'

It has 'nineteen mouths' – *ekonavimshati mukhah*. These are all descriptions of the 'organs' by which the first quarter of the 'Supreme Being' functions in the *jagrita avastha* or in the waking state. He recognizes the world and deals with it through the 'nineteen mouths,' meaning, 'that by which the world is absorbed.' This is not counted arithmetically – it is just to show how important the organs are and how they are related to the waking state of man's existence. The 'nineteen mouths' are the five senses, the five organs of activity, the five breaths, the mind, the intellect, the consciousness and the ego.

The five senses are: sight, hearing, smell, taste and touch.

The five organs of activity are: the organ of speech – *vaak*; the organs of action – the hands to do things; the organs of locomotion – the feet to move; the organs of generation, without which all evolution would come to a halt; the organs of excretion – to eliminate the toxic wastes.

The five vital breaths are: *prana, apaana, vyaana, udaana* and *samaana* – different kinds of life currents.

The *manas* – the mind – which is made up of feelings and emotions. The *buddhi* – the intellect – emotions and intellect are separated.

The *ahamkara* – the ego – the feeling of being 'myself', the basic feeling of 'I am.' When I wake up in the morning, before I open my eyes I feel, 'I exist.' Only if I exist does the world exist! When I go to sleep, what exists as far as I am concerned? Nothing! Of course, the world is there but it does not exist as long as I am sleeping!

The *chitta* – conciousness – thus making a total of nineteen.

All these together make up what is mentioned here as the 'nineteen mouths' of that 'Being,' which represents the *jagrita avastha*, the waking state whose function is to cognize and co-relate with the physical world.

And what does It enjoy? It enjoys the material objects; It experiences the material world and enjoys it. So It is called *sthula bhukh* – 'That which enjoys material objects.'

It is called *vaishwanara* because It is 'that which takes along all beings of the universe.' It is that which leads all of us towards enjoyment. Due to it we all have the in-built tendency to enjoy. Therefore, It is called *vaishwanara prathama paada* – that is the first quarter of that 'Supreme Being.'

Now, when we say 'enjoy,' we must go a little deeper into what we mean by it. All sane human beings have a desire to enjoy. There is nothing wrong with that. The desire to enjoy is our innate tendency because it is the characteristic of the 'Supreme Being.'

The 'Supreme Being' has been defined as 'Bliss' in the *Upanishads*. Those who have evolved spiritually also experience this. It is the *pramaana*, or the proof that the essential characteristic of the 'Supreme Being' is *ananda* – Bliss! This is not merely because the *Shruti* says so but because of one's *anubhava*, one's experience. *Sat Chit Ananda Murti*, is one of the descriptions of the 'Supreme Being.' *Sat* means 'Truth,' ever-existing Truth' because it is permanent, while everything else is temporary. It is called *Chit* because it is of the nature of 'Consciousness.' And it is *Ananda* because it is, by its very nature, full of 'Bliss'!

All human beings, deep down in their minds, are looking for ultimate happiness. This 'looking for bliss' is a common factor in all of us. We call it 'the search for happiness.' There is an innate longing for happiness in us. Every movement in civilization is towards that. Indeed, the very act of human creation is because of 'Bliss' and not just 'wanting to procreate.'

But somewhere along the line, we find ourselves looking for it in the wrong place, in the wrong direction. We are not guided properly and have therefore not looked in the right direction. What is the right direction?

First, we must be told, and we must understand, that we are all a 'spark' of that 'Supreme Being.' We must understand that the Bliss we are looking for can be found only in communication with that 'Supreme Being' because that 'Supreme Being' is, in its essence, Bliss!

Kabirdas illustrates this in his famous story about the musk-deer, which has *kasturi* or musk in a little bag behind its tail. In the breeding season, it exudes a lovely fragrance of *kasturi*. This poor deer goes around looking for the source of the fragrance all over the place, not knowing that it has only to redirect its attention to itself! So too, this fragrance is there in man, and the essence of that fragrance is the 'Supreme Being.' Not knowing the essence of that fragrance and its source, we look around for it! This is the mechanism that has been built by the 'Supreme Being' so that the world continues to evolve.

We all look for happiness endlessly in the material world. 'If I have one crore of rupees, then I would be happier with two crores! If I enjoy something once, I need more of it to enjoy!' Some 'realized' people understand that this process of seeking happiness through external sources is unending. They have learnt this truth either by seeing others' experiences or through their own. One does not have to put one's own finger into the fire to know that it burns!

All are looking for happiness, for bliss – there is nothing wrong with that. Only, they seek it in the wrong direction. Somewhere along the line we must ask ourselves, 'Can a search for material happiness ever end?'

Bliss is the essential characteristic of the 'Supreme Being' which is inherent in all of us. We have only to turn around and go back to the source. And the source for every living being has to be only himself. It cannot be outside. Thus the message of the *Upanishad* is that the 'Supreme Being' is not something that is remote, far off. It is very near, close to you, within you, and It is of the nature of Bliss.

Among the Sufis there is a saying – 'He is nearer to you than your own jugular vein.' Your jugular vein is the nearest part of you, nothing can be closer. 'He is nearer to you than your own jugular vein.' Even before we think, He knows! That which stimulates thought is itself the 'Supreme Being'!

We cannot take God for granted. We cannot go before the picture of God and say, 'Look God! I am a good man, I have always prayed to you, why am I suffering?' God knows what we are. We cannot be hypocrites and say, 'Look, I don't like this world, take me away!' And when the time comes to be really 'taken away,' we get frightened and run for our lives!

There is a story of an old lady who used to go to the temple everyday and cry before the deity, 'O Goddess, why don't you take me

away? What do I have to do now in this world? Everything is over...'
and so on. The priest of the temple got fed up of this lady coming
and making a scene everyday. So one day he went and stood behind
the many-armed deity. When the lady approached and said, 'Take
me away!,' he raised his hands and said, 'Come!' She ran for her life
screaming, 'What do you mean? I have to look after my great grand-
son when he returns from school!' The material and emotional pull
of this world is unending!

Sometimes we believe we are cursed by fate. But what we consider a curse may turn out to be a blessing. Not knowing the entire
plan, the whole scheme of things, we get agitated. As time goes by
we discover that this state of being 'cursed' or 'blessed' is not permanent. Then we listen to somebody telling us in a *satsang*, or we
read a book or scripture that says, 'There is 'something' permanent
but it is not 'this.' There is something else that is very blissful. That
is to know the Lord Himself, the 'Supreme Being.' You are a spark
of that 'Supreme Being' and therefore, bliss is a part of your being!
One can find the Truth through meditation, through understanding, through reading scriptures, through a teacher. Different religions give different ways. Different *sadhanas* have been prescribed
for different kinds of people depending on the person, his field of
activity, and the times he lives in.

So, we have discussed the *jagrita sthana* – the first quarter of that
supreme *aum*, which is represented by 'A,' whose duty or work is
'to recognize' external objects – *bahish prajnah*; whose sphere of
activity is the waking state – *jagrita avastha*; who has seven limbs
– *saptaanga* and nineteen mouths – *ekonavimshati mukhah*; who
enjoys material objects – *sthula bhukh;* and who is known as *vaishwanara.*

SHLOKA 4

*swapna sthaano antah prajnah saptaanga ekonavimshati mukhah
pravivikta bhukh taijaso dwitiyah paadah.*

This is the second quarter of that Supreme *aum*, which is 'U.' It is *taijasa*, which means, 'conscious of the internal.' *Vaishwanara* was 'conscious of the external,' whereas *taijasa* is 'conscious of the inner.' It illumines the inner. Its sphere of activity is *swapna*. It cognizes internally – *swapna sthaano antah prajnah*. It also has seven limbs – *saptaanga* – because whatever the physical body has, the dream body has too. It has also 'nineteen mouths' by which it enjoys. It enjoys that which is subtle – *pravivikta bhukh*. *Vaishwanara* enjoys the gross objects, whereas *taijasa* enjoys the subtle ones. This subtle enjoyment is the second part – *dwitiya paada* – of that Supreme *aum*.

In the discussions that follow, we will go into the second quarter – the dream, the third quarter – deep sleep, and then the fourth and most important – *turiya*, represented by the last part – *ardha matra*. When one has finished chanting *aum*, the sound that slowly disappears – that vibration, that part is called *turiya*.

To repeat the salient points covered so far –

The *Mandukya Upanishad*, like all other *Upanishads*, is a scripture meant for understanding the meaning of the 'Supreme Reality.' The *Upanishads* refer to it as 'Brahman.' What is its connection with us human beings who are called *jeevatma*? How are we related to that 'Supreme Being'? What is it that the scriptures talk about regarding that 'Supreme Being'?

The *Mandukya Upanishad* is very short, consisting of only twelve *shlokas*. It takes up the discussion of the 'Supreme Being' as *aum*. The 'Supreme Being' is referred to in many places in the *Vedas* and the *Upanishads* as the *pranava* – *aum*. Considering the 'Supreme Being' as symbolized by *aum*, the *rishi* describes how *aum* is divided into four parts – 'A,' 'U' and 'M' being the three syllables that make *aum*, and the '… mmm …' vibration being the fourth part, each part symbolizing a particular function of the 'Supreme Being.'

As the first *shloka* says,

aum ityetad aksharam idam sarvam tasyopa vyaakhyaanam
bhutam bhavam bhavishyaditi sarvam aumkaara eva
yacchaanyat trikaalateetam tadapyo aumkaara eva.

That supreme syllable 'aum,' which is a representation of the 'Supreme Being' is all this. Therefore, nothing is beyond the scope of that Supreme Being. Everything is in the 'Supreme Being' and the Supreme Being is in everything! All that is past, present and future is in the Supreme Being. This is the difference between the human and the Supreme, because the human being cannot think in terms of the past, present and future at the same time. We have only a memory of the past; we can only speculate about the future. The past is a memory in the form of pictures, thought-forms. The future is imagination, again in the form of pictures, thought-forms. The only thing we know is the present.

In contrast, the Supreme *aum* or *Brahman*, knows the present, past and the future at the same time! The human mind and the human brain cannot have a concept of this as it is beyond their capacity. The *Upanishad* also says that, apart from what is within the scope of time, meaning the past, present and future, anything which is beyond that, not conditioned by time, that is timeless, that also is the 'Supreme *Brahman*,' the supreme syllable *aum*.

The second *shloka* says, 'All this is verily *Brahman*' – *sarvam hyetad brahma*. There is nothing that can be said to be 'not *Brahman*.' '*Brahman*' is the term used by the *Upanishad* to mean 'The Supreme Reality.'

The next sentence is *ayam atma brahma* – 'This *atma* is *Brahman*.' The word *atma* is introduced here to show that we are not talking about an abstraction; we are talking about a 'Being' – *atma*. So this *Brahman*, which is beyond time, is a 'Being,' not just an abstract idea or an ideal. 'That *atma* is *Brahman*' or 'that *Brahman* is *atma*.'

Then, *soyam atma chatushpaad:* This *atma*, which is *Brahman*, is divided into four quarters or four parts. The first part is called, *vaishwanara* whose sphere of activity is *jagrita avastha* – the waking state.

In this *Upanishad*, *aum* represents the 'Supreme Being.' The 'A' represents the first quarter or the waking state. *Jagrita sthaano bahish prajnah* – that means the quality or the capacity to recognize the objects in the outside world. It is a representation of the 'Supreme Being' as the *viraat purusha* with its head being the heaven, feet being the earth, and so on – they are the 'seven limbs'. It has 'nineteen mouths' which include the five sense organs, five organs of action, five vital breaths, the mind, intellect, consciousness and ego, the sense of 'I-ness'.

It is called *vaishwanara* because it is that part of the 'Supreme Being' in the 'wakeful state' – *jagrita sthaana* who operates in the sphere of wakefulness ; who leads us all to the enjoyment of objects. That is the first part – *prathama paada*. So, the first part or the *jagrita* is conscious of the outside, the material world. It recognizes the external objects; it cognizes the outside world and deals with it.

The *Upanishads* deal with the common experiences of all human beings, irrespective of caste, creed or religion. We do not have to believe in God to know that we are awake, we dream and we have deep sleep. These three experiences are common to all! Deep sleep helps us to relax and forget everything about this world, which is why we feel refreshed when we wake up.

The second part is called the 'dream state'. *Swapna sthaano antah prajnah saptaanga ekonavimshati mukhah pravivikta bhukh taijaso dwitiyah paadah.*

The second part, which is represented by 'U' or 'O' sound of *aum*, is called *taijasa*. *Taijasa* means 'conscious'. The *swapna avastha*, the dream state, is also called *taijasa* because it is like a light that shines in a closed place. In a dream, our eyes are closed and so we do not see the outside light; but we do see light, we see the day, night and various other things. All this is illumined by the *taijasa*, the second part of the 'Supreme Being'.

Although the 'Supreme Being' cannot be split up into parts, this is a convenient way of describing that the 'U' of *aum* symbolizes the dream state which is common to all human beings. Its sphere of activity is the dream state and its function is to recognize internal objects. It also has the 'seven limbs' and the 'nineteen mouths' and so on, because even in the dream state we enjoy, eat, drink and do various things. So all the organs are there, but in a different form, a more subtle form, and so it enjoys experiences of subtle objects as opposed to the gross objects that is enjoyed by the *jagrita* in the *jagrita sthaana*.

Now, these dream experiences need not be dismissed as unreal. In fact, when the dream takes place, at that moment the dream state is as real as the waking state. Only when we wake up from the dream does it become unreal; otherwise it is as real as the reality of the outside world! When you are chased by a tiger in a dream, you are actually being chased by a tiger in that state. It cannot be doubted. When you wake up, your heart is still beating fast, you are sweating, your body is trembling. It has the same effect on the mind and the physical body as in the waking state. So it is as real in the dream state as it would be in the waking state!

There is a little explanatory story in which the great sage Rajarishi Janaka had in which he was a beggar going around in rags with a begging bowl, suffering a lot of misery and hunger. Then he wakes up and realizes he is in his palace, lying in his bed!

He is confused. He has a question to ask the great sage Yajnavalkya, who is his Guru. He asks him, 'Sir, please answer this question – am I a beggar or am I a king? Because, being a beggar was a very real experience! If my dream had stretched on for long and I had not waken up from that state, then I would have continued that beggar's existence. Now that I have woken up I can say that it is a dream. So please tell me, what am I in reality? Where do I anchor myself?'

This is how the dream state is; it is real and it is an experience of the subtle world, the inner world of imagination and thoughts. Many a time, what is not fulfilled in our waking state may be fulfilled in the dream. Sometimes, bottled-up emotions and desires, long forgotten or suppressed, may surface in the form of dreams.

This *taijasa*, or dream state, has a way of inventing its own world which is similar to day-dreaming. Sometimes, in the waking state, we sit down and imagine various things. At that time, most of our mind is in the *jagrita sthaana* and so we are able to recognize this activity as an imagination or visualization, but in *swapna*, the *jagrita* or the waking state is held in abeyance. It is 'closed.' So the *swapna* becomes real.

Now, we move on to the third quarter of the four parts – deep-sleep.

SHLOKA 5

*yatra supto na kanchan kaamam kaamayate na
kanchan swapnam pashyati tat sushuptam.
sushupta sthaana eki bhutah prajnana ghana
eva anandamay hy aananda bukh cheto mhukah
praajnas tritiyah paadah.*

The third part of that 'Supreme Being' *aum* is called the *prajna*, which is identified with the sound 'M' of *aum*. It is identified with the last sound 'M' where in everything is 'closed' and absorbed in itself. When *aum* is chanted, it finishes with the closing of the mouth. If one wants to produce a fresh sound, the mouth has to be opened again. So, it represents the 'closing up' or the end of all activity, where both the waking-activity of the mind represented by 'A' and the dream-activity represented by 'U', are in abeyance. They are all drawn in, like a tortoise pulling in its head and limbs. The energies that are operating, both in the physical world and the dream or the subtle world, have ceased to function; everything is 'closed' and absorbed in itself. That state is called *sushupti*.

In that state, when one is fast asleep, one has no desire – *kaama*. One does not have any desire since there is nothing and nobody existing in that state to desire or to be desired. Everything is rolled-up, coiled-up! 'It does not see any dreams.' There is not even a desire for dreams.

Tat sushuptam – that is called *sushuptam*. *Sushuptasthaana eki bhutah* – means all differences have ceased, all is rolled into one, there is only one. Differences between the 'seer' and the 'seen' have ceased; differences between the 'subject' and 'object' have ceased; it does not cognize anything. This is deep sleep. There is only one mass of consciousness. It is called *prajna* in this particular section. As *jagrita* it is called *vaishwanara*, as *swapna* it is called *taijasa* and as *sushupti* it is called *prajna*. So, as *prajna* in the *sushupta avastha*, is in absolute rest. There is no outward movement as was seen in *vaishwanara* in the *jagrita avastha*, and there is no inward movement as was seen in *taijasa*, in the *swapna avastha*.

It is just enjoying itself – *ananda bhukhah*. It is an enjoyer of happiness. That is called *prajna*, and that is the *tritiya paada* – the third part, 'M' of the 'Supreme Being,' symbolized as *aum*.

So, absolute bliss is being enjoyed in deep sleep. The only difference is that one is not even aware of the enjoyment of that Supreme Bliss. But there is enjoyment going on because, when we wake up, we always feel, 'Ah! I had a wonderful sleep! It was very restful!'

Deep sleep is the greatest blessing that has been given to us. It is in this *sushupta avastha* that we go to rest finally, after a whole day of activity, and even after the dream state has ended. And because there is no outward or inward movement, there is no wastage of energy of any kind.

There is also no differentiation between 'me' and 'you' because in deep sleep I am not aware of anything. Since there is no 'I' and 'you,' there is no duality. Since there is no duality, there is no tension, no insecurity, no friction. As long as there is duality, there is no rest, no peace.

I might go to sleep clutching my safe-keys in my hand because I am afraid you may come and rob my safe, but when I am in deep-sleep it does not matter, because there is no discrimination and duality, there is no fear but absolute rest. So, when I wake up from deep sleep, I feel absolutely refreshed. *Jagrita, swapna* and *sushupti* are all parts of that 'Supreme Being.'

SHLOKA 6

*aesha sarveshwara aesha sarvajnah aesho antaryaami
aesha yonih sarvasya prabhavaapyayau hi bhutanaam.*

Which means, that 'Being,' who is in absolute bliss, who is free from all dualities, who is now in the state of *sushupti,* that 'Being' is really 'The Lord of all' – *aesha sarveshwara.* The *rishi* talks about that 'Supreme Being' as *prajna.* It is the 'Lord of all.' However, that 'Being' is beyond the mind, so we cannot conceive of it with our brains. But that does not mean that it is an abstract entity. A Lord cannot be an abstract entity. It is a 'Being' and that is why the word, *sarveshwara* – 'the Lord,' is used. You cannot use the term 'Lord' for magnetic energy or for nuclear energy!

Aesha sarveshwara aesha sarvajnah – 'It knows everything; The knower of All.' It is Omniscient. It also means that when we say 'I know' we are mistaken. It is only the 'Supreme Being' who knows, and it is because our consciousness is an *amsha,* a part, of the 'Supreme Being,' that we know! Therefore, when we say, 'I know,' it is wrong. That is what the *Upanishads* have said. The *Kena Upanishad* for instance, says, 'He who thinks he knows, knows not, and he who knows not, knows!' This is not a riddle. It is to indicate that with our limited intellect, if we think we know the 'Supreme Being,' we are still groveling in darkness. When it is completely understood that it cannot be known, then it comes as a flash which is beyond our understanding. So it is this 'Supreme Being' who is the 'Lord of all – the knower of all.' It is also *aesho antaryaami* – our 'inner controller.'

From this deep sleep, in which there is no outward or inward recognition, arises the waking-state; that consciousness, which was blissfully present without any duality, begins to take on the modes of duality; then life begins again, interaction begins again with the outside world.

It is also *aesha yonih* – 'The Source' – the *yoni* of all creation. All creation proceeds from this; it is the beginning and the end of all beings.

In the Bhagavad Gita also, when Krishna talks about the 'Supreme Being' as represented in Himself, He says, *'Aham atma gudakesha sarva bhutaakshya sthithahaa aham aadishcha madhyam cha bhutaanam antah eva cha.'*

Arjuna is referred to as *gudakesha* which means, 'the conqueror of sleep.' That does not mean that *Arjuna* does not sleep! 'Sleep' here represents 'ignorance' – the 'Sleep of ignorance.' So, *gudakesha* is the one who is seeing, who is wide awake in knowledge. Krishna says, 'Do understand, O Arjuna, my true essence ; do not mistake me for the body. In my true essence – *aham aadishcha madhyam cha bhutaanam antah eva cha* – I am the beginning, the middle and the end of everything!'

This *Upanishad* also calls It, *sarvasya prabhavaapyayau hi bhutaanaam* – 'It is the beginning and the end of all beings.'

When we chant, *'aum,'* there is a vibration that goes on and on. *'aum….mm….mm…'* – That sound is represented in Sanskrit by a small crescent shape with a dot – it is not a letter; it is called *ardha maatra*. That represents the essence, the 'Ultimate Reality' from which all the other states come about. That is called *turiya*.

And why has it been differentiated and given after *sushupti*? It is because *turiya* is the state or sphere of activity of the 'Supreme Being' which is not commonly experienced by all human beings. One in a million may experience *turiya*. It should not be mistaken that the 'Supreme Being' who is included in the three *maatras* of *aum* – 'A,' 'U' and 'M' – is only involved in the waking, dream and deep sleep states. True, the three *maatras* are the parts of that 'Supreme Being.' But the 'Supreme Being' is not made of these parts – it is beyond that. To prove that, *turiya* has been separated.

It is 'That' which cannot be expressed by any word in any language. It is inexpressible. That 'Supreme Being' is represented by the last sound. For instance, when we strike the bell, it goes on and on and on. Nobody knows where it ends. The sound has not gone anywhere – it is still there, but its vibrations have become so subtle now, that the ear cannot sense it. There may be creatures that can still hear it, if they are sensitive to these subtle frequencies. Therefore, the sound is unending.

That 'unending sound' symbolizes the *turiya* state of that 'Supreme Being' which cannot be grasped by the intellect. So, we should not think that the 'Supreme Being,' the *Brahman* of the *Upanishad*, is only confined to the states which we all experience and are aware of – the waking, dream and deep sleep states. These states are only part of that 'Supreme Being' which also lies beyond these states.

SHLOKA 7

na antah prajnam na bahish prajnam nobhayatah prajnam
na prajnaanaghanam na prajnam naa prajnam.
adrishtam avyavahaaryam agraahyam alakshanam achintyam
avyapadeshyam ekaatma pratyayasaaram prapanchopashamam shaan-
tam shivam advaitam chaturtham manyantey sa atmaa sa vijneyah.

So *turiya* is represented as the fourth quarter of the 'Supreme Being,' as the *ardha maatra* – 'that is to be known' – *sa vijneyah*. It may sound like a contradiction because the Supreme Being has also been described as *alakshanam achintyam agraahyam*. *Agraahyam* means 'that which cannot be grasped,' yet the last words of this *shloka* are *sa vijneyah* – 'that is to be known.' How can one know 'that which cannot be grasped?' However, It is not a contradiction, as we will see.

About *turiya* it was said, 'It is not that which cognizes both internal and external objects.' Note that it is not said 'does not'; it is said 'is not' that which cognizes internal or external objects. It is not a mass of cognition like the *sushupti*. It is not cognitive, and yet not noncognitive. It is 'unseen' – *adrishtam*. 'It cannot be seen,' which means, the physical eyes cannot see it – like air, which we cannot see with our eyes and yet we know exists.

It is *avyavahaaryam* – 'That which cannot be spoken of,' because words fail to explain what it is. There is not enough praise for it. There is no word by which it can be exactly described. It is beyond all words.

It is *agraahyam* – 'ungraspable.' That means, it cannot be grasped either by the physical senses in the waking state, or in the dream state, nor can it be grasped in deep sleep. Therefore it is called 'ungraspable.'

It is *alakshanam* – 'without any distinctive marks.' There is no 'physical distinctive mark' or *lakshanam*, by which it can be identified using our physical senses.

It is *achintyam* –'unthinkable' – which means, it does not fit into any of our thoughts or our ways of thinking. In fact, the actions of the 'Supreme Being' also cannot be fitted into our logical process of thinking. Our logical process is, 'one plus one is two.' Perhaps it is akin to the title of an old Hindi movie called *Do Aur Do Panch* – 'two plus two is five'! If you read higher Physics, perhaps you will understand this. In quantum physics we learn of the principle of uncertainty which states that the properties of a particle cannot be determined or known with certainty at the micro level. From the 'absolute certainty' of ignorance we arrive at the 'uncertainty' of knowledge – a great discovery, a great step forward!

Here the *Upanishad* says, 'It is *agraahyam*' – 'that which cannot be conceived of or grasped' which means, however much we try to grasp it, our human brain is not capable of conceiving it. It is the essence of the knowledge of our own 'Self.' It is because of this essence that our 'Self' is able to cognize, to be conscious and is able to act in the waking, dream and deep sleep states.

It is into 'That' that the whole world is resolved when the world has completely disappeared, when all thinking and all desire are 'closed up.' What is our world? Our world is the desire-prompted movement of any living being towards happiness! This is our only movement in the whole of evolution. There is no other. Any discovery or progress always evolved to make man happier!

When all movements have stopped and resolved in the *turiya*, in that 'Supreme Being,' then, That Is! That is the state when all desires have ceased, when all resolutions have gone except for one, to remain in that state, in that calmness. It is into that 'Supreme Being' that the whole mental, physical and psychological worlds are resolved.

It is *shaantam* – absolute peace. That *prajna* is the height, the zenith of all peace. The *Upanishad* stresses that it is not an abstract idea but concrete, because:

- It is *shivam*, it is 'auspicious, benign, compassionate.'
- It is *advaitam*, it is 'non-dual,' which means that there is only one *prajna*, there is only one 'Supreme Being.' There is no duality. There may be other entities, other agents, but only one 'Supreme Being'. You may call it by any name.

There is an incident connected with one of the well-known Shankaracharyas of the Sringeri Peeth – Sri Chandrashekhar Bharati Swami. He was so deep into the actual experience of the spiritual 'Truth' that even the people inside the *mutt* – ashram, could not understand him. Some thought he was suffering from some mental disorder. One day, two men came to him and had a discussion. One man believed in the Lord as Narayana – he was a Vaishnava; and the other believed in the Lord as Shiva – he was a Shaiva.

The *Acharya* asked one man, 'Tell me, is there one Supreme God or many?' The man replied, 'There is only one Supreme God.' He then asked the other man, 'What do you say?' He said, 'Yes, there is only one Supreme God, not many.' The *Acharya* said,

'So you both agree! Only, you call Him Shiva, and you call Him Narayana!' The first man said, 'But, there is only one Supreme Being – Narayana, not Shiva!' The other man protested, 'No! No! It is Shiva and none other!' The *Acharya* said, 'Now listen! At this moment, in my present state, I see only the lotus feet of the Lord! All of us are in that state. So, let us continue with that and when we are advanced enough to see His face, then we can decide whether the *namam* (the caste mark worn on the forehead by orthodox Hindus) is horizontal or vertical!' (Believers in Narayana have vertical caste marks, believers in Shiva have horizontal caste marks on their forehead).

So, it is *shaantam, shivam, advaitam*. There is only 'One,' peaceful and compassionate; there is no duality in it. The wise men of old believe that this is the fourth part of that 'Supreme Being.'

Sa atma – 'that is the Self' – 'the true Self'.

Sa vijneya – 'that is to be understood,' 'that is to be known.'

All the above descriptions are pointers towards knowing the Self and so, if you see anything which does not conform to the description of *prajna*, then it cannot be the 'Supreme Being.' The psychological aspect is that it has to be always accompanied by *shaantam* – peace, absolute peace. The Sufis call it *salaamat* – absolute peace.

SHLOKA 8

soyam atma adhyaksharam aumkaaraardhimatram paada maatra maatrascha paada akaara ukaara makaara iti.

Which means: 'this is the 'Self,' this is the *atman*, which is of the nature of the syllable *aum*; the quarters are its elements. The elements are the syllables 'A,' 'U' and 'M.' And this we have described.

Thus the eighth *shloka* of the Upanishad summarises what has gone before.

SHLOKA 9

jagrita sthaano vaishwanaro akaarah prathama maatra aapter adimatvad
vaapnoti ha vai sarvaankaaman aadischa bhavati ya evam veda.

The *vaishwanara*, the first quarter of the Supreme Being' whose sphere of activity is the waking state, is represented by the letter 'A, the first element. 'A' is derived from the root '*ap*,' which means 'to obtain.' 'A' is also the first letter of the alphabet – *akshara*. 'A' is the first sound that anyone, including a dumb person, can make! So 'A' represents the *jagrita avastha*, the waking state or the first quarter of the 'Supreme Being.' 'He who knows this, the one who understands this, fulfils all desires.' The one who understands that all the activity of the waking state is just the first quarter of the 'Supreme Being' becomes the first, which means, he recognizes the first in himself. He obtains an immeasurable capacity to work and attain goals. He understands that the spark of the 'Supreme Being' which is within him, has vast capacities, which are beyond the concept of the limited human brain, and therefore 'he becomes the first.' That is one meaning.

The other meaning is that by understanding that the waking state is after all only a small part of the 'Supreme Being,' he begins to think that it is better to understand the whole 'Supreme Being' who is all the four quarters! Whereas, by understanding only the waking quarter, he attains only the first step – one small part of the 'Supreme Being.'

By understanding the *Upanishad* and realizing that this is only one quarter of that 'Supreme Being,' while the whole 'Supreme Being' is to be known in *turiya*, he becomes the first, he becomes the most eminent of all persons.

SHLOKA 10

swapna sthaanas taijasa ukaaro dwitiya
maatrotkarshaad ubhayat vaadvot karshati ha vaijnana santatim
samaanascha bhavati naasya brahma vit kulay bhavati ya evam veda.

The second quarter of the 'Supreme Being' whose sphere of activity is the dream state, is the *taijasa*. It is represented by the letter 'U,' which is the second element. It is the second because it is intermediate, between the first and the third. When we chant *aum*, the 'A' sound starts from the throat. Then we lengthen it to 'U,' when it comes to the middle of the tongue, and it is followed by 'M,' when it comes to the end of the mouth. So, it is intermediate.

'U' is the intermediate, and so it represents the intermediate. 'He who knows this exults in the continuity of knowledge and he becomes equal.' That means, by understanding that the dream state or *taijasa* is only the intermediate quarter of the 'Supreme Being,' he gains the knowledge in continuity, which means, he does not stop there; he continues to move until he reaches the understanding of *sushupti*. And then, from there, it is a step to *turiya*!

Naasya brahma vit kulay bhavati ya evam veda. – 'In his family is born no one who does not know the *Brahman*.' That means, if one person in the family understands the different quarters of the 'Supreme Being' and experiences it through proper *sadhana*, under the guidance of a teacher, his whole family benefits.

The *Upanishads* only talk about the Truth. In fact, the *Upanishads* are taught only to the *aaptas*, meaning, 'those who are fit to receive it.' A student was fit to receive it only after he had first gone through all the training that was necessary as a *brahmachari*, in the ancient *gurukulas*, or schools. For years, he had to study the *shastras*, chant the *Gayatri*, do intense *sadhana* and lead a pure life, until he came to the stage when the *Upanishads* could be taught to him. If such a person understands the import of this *Upanishad*, then, 'in his family, no one is born who is not the knower of the Brahman.' But that is very rare. Theoretically, one can be a *pundit* and know a lot of *Upanishads*, but to understand the *Upanishad* means to experience it, and for that a teacher is necessary; one has to go through *sadhana*.

In the period of intense study as a *brahmachari*, one's mind and energies are completely focused on the indepth understanding of that subject. Only after that does one begin to realize the truth of the *Upanishads*. It is not that everyone should remain a *brahmachari* and become a *sanyasi* afterwards. One is allowed to become a *grihasta* and progress slowly. However, it is not so easy. Even in the *Upanishads*, you will find the disciple asks the teacher a question; the master answers. The disciple goes through it, thinks about it, and comes back with his conclusion. The master guides him with further questions and asks him to think well on what *Brahman* is. This process continues until the disciple eliminates everything and realizes what *Brahman*, the 'Supreme Being,' is.

In the family of such a realised person, 'nobody will be born who is not a knower of *Brahman*.'

SHLOKA 11

sushuptasthaanah prajno makaarastritiya maatra miterapiterva minoti ha va idam sarvam apeetish cha bhavati ya evam veda.

The third element 'M,' whose sphere of activity is the state of deep sleep is called *prajna*, the third quarter of the 'Supreme Being.'

Now, '*im*', which is the root of the sound 'M,' can either mean 'to merge' or 'to measure.' 'To measure' means 'to measure the entire universe.'

There is a lovely story in the Puranas of Maha Vishnu, who in the Vaman Avatar, came to the demon-king Maha Bali and asked for a boon. He asked for as much land as would be covered by his three foot steps. Maha Bali agreed. The Lord took two steps, spanning the entire earth with one, and the entire sky with the other! Since there was no space left for the third footstep, Maha Bali offered his own head for the Lord to place His foot. That 'Supreme Being' who can measure everything out, is immeasurable Himself!

The root *im* also means 'to merge.' Everything merges into It and becomes one whole. He who knows and understands this, also merges all unto himself. *Sarvam apeetischa bhavati ya evam veda* –

'He who knows this, merges everything in himself and remains in absolute peace'.

SHLOKA 12

amaatraschaturtho avyavahaaryam prapanchopashamaha shivo advaita evam aumkaara atmaiva samvishaty atmana atmaanam ya evam veda.

The fourth part – the *turiya* – which has no elements, which cannot be spoken of, and into which the whole world is resolved, that *aum* is the 'Self'. *Aum* is auspicious, benign, non-dual. It is the 'Real Self' of everything. 'He who knows this, enters that 'Supreme Self' with his 'Self'. He who knows this, realizes that the 'Supreme Being' is spread out in this world as *sarvam*, as everything, and yet It remains separate and untouched by anything in this world.

There is a particular description used for this – *achintya bheda abheda*, which means 'identity and duality together'. That is being 'One' and at the same time, being different. This cannot be conceived by our brain. We can only think of either 'being together' or 'not together'. But the 'Supreme Being' is not like us. The 'Supreme Being' can be 'together' or 'not together' at the same time! That is Its uniqueness!

Some people say 'the Supreme Being has no form'. Others say 'the Supreme Being has form'. If indeed the Supreme Being is infinite, all-powerful, how can we decide whether it has a form or not? We simply cannot decide!

Lord Dakshinamurthi is depicted sitting with his legs folded and his hand in a particular pose, with the thumb meeting the forefinger, called the *Chinmudra*. Lord Dakshinamurthi is silent. He never speaks, but by this *mudra* he teaches. Those who understand, realize that it is a symbol which means that the 'Supreme Self' depicted by the thumb, and the 'Supreme Being' depicted by the forefinger, are one and the same, because the two are joined to form a circle. They are not different. That 'Supreme Being' which is in me and that 'Supreme Being' which is in you, when we see both as one – 'One whole' – then, all that is left is *Sat Chit Ananda* depicted by the three extended fingers. *Sat* – meaning 'the Truth'; *Chit* – meaning 'absolute consciousness'; and *Ananda* – meaning 'complete bliss,' towards which all of us are moving.

The tendency to enjoy and move towards happiness is an essential part of our soul, of our being. The only problem is that the search for this happiness is in the 'wrong' or 'different' direction. If only the direction can be changed and brought back to the source of all happiness, which is the 'Supreme Being,' then all problems and doubts will be resolved.

Let me repeat the interesting story by Kabirdas about the *kasturi mriga* – the musk deer. The *kasturi mriga* has a small bag of *kasturi*, musk, somewhere behind its tail. During the breeding season when it exudes the fragrance of *kasturi*, the poor deer, not knowing where this fragrance emanates from, goes around searching for it everywhere until it gets all scratched and bleeding. This story puts the problem in a nutshell.

The fragrance is in all of us. It is the source of all creation. Unlike the musk deer, we humans have become evolved; we can search and find the source of this fragrance. But we search for happiness in the material world until somebody points out, 'Now, watch it! Halt, turn back! To find the Source from which all this comes, turn within!' And then one turns within and gradually learns to commune with the 'Supreme Being.' That is the aim of life! And to reach that aim one has to change direction.

Like every high aim, the search for happiness within oneself requires *sadhana*, patience and hard work, because nothing can be achieved without that. Sadly, it is only in religious and spiritual matters that people want a short cut. For everything else, like making money or gaining fame, we are ready to work hard without any problem! But there is no short cut in spiritual matters! For spiritual development, one does not have to run away from day-to-day life. One can remain in the material world. With proper guidance, one can also advance spiritually. The search must be done with humility, because if we think we already know, then we are not going to learn anything. Soon, everybody can become a teacher.

There is a beautiful book called the 'Avadhoota Gita.' It is a little abstract. What is interesting in that book is that the *avadhoota* says he has twenty-four *Gurus*. He says that he learns different things from different people, and also from other beings, including the bees. He says, 'The honeybee too is my *Guru*, because it teaches me how to save for a rainy day.'

This honeybee reminds me of the ancient tradition, when monks had to beg from door to door for food. They used to gather just a handful from each house because they did not want to tax the householder. That particular mode of *bhiksha* was called *madhukari* which means collecting food like the bee which goes from flower to flower gathering nectar from here and there and putting it all together. What a lovely word, '*madhukari*'! Perhaps such *bhiksha* may also taste like honey! In those days, food was given with the proper attitude. Nowadays it would be difficult to find such householders – you could get the door slammed on your face!

The *Manu Smriti* gives the code of conduct for the householder to follow in order to live ideally. It is interesting to note that when the food is ready, the head of the household is supposed to go out to the gate of the house and shout loudly three times, 'Is anyone hungry here?' The first person who responds to this should be invited home and fed; then the householder should eat what remains. It is such a wonderful principle. What an attitude it inspires!

All this comes about when one realizes that the 'Divine Supreme Being' is innate in all beings. Then, the whole world becomes your family!

To sum up, the *Mandukya Upanishad* basically deals with the subject of *aum* and the three states of consciousness that are connected with *aum*, the 'Supreme Being.'

Aum Shantih, Shantih, Shantih!

Printed in Great Britain
by Amazon

28738336R00096